RecruitCONSULT!
Leadership

The Corporate Talent Acquisition

Leader's Field Book

Second Edition

Jeremy M. Eskenazi

STAR
STRATEGIC TALENT
ACQUISITION ROUNDTABLE
PRESS

Cover Design: Wendy White

Interior Design and Illustrations: Chris Derrick

Editor: Dianne Tennen

Indexing: Rose Ippolito

Research: Miranda Horton

Editorial Proofreading: John Carrozza, Brad Loewen, Miranda Horton

CONTENTS

ABOUT THE AUTHOR

Jeremy Eskenazi is currently the Managing Principal of Riviera Advisors, Inc. a boutique Human Resources consulting firm that he founded in 2001. Riviera Advisors partners with organizations globally to improve and enhance their ability to attract and hire talent. Jeremy draws on more than 30 years of experience and expertise to help companies assess and enhance their talent management systems and processes.

Prior to founding Riviera Advisors, Jeremy served as Vice President, Talent Acquisition for Idealab, the world's premier technology business incubator. Jeremy's role encompassed building and leading a global team in the development and delivery of recruiting, university relations, and executive search services to Idealab's more than 30 network companies.

Jeremy came to Idealab after serving as Director of Talent Acquisition for Amazon.com. In this role, Jeremy led all talent acquisition and recruiting activities for this high-growth global organization. Later, Jeremy served in the role of Vice President, Strategic Growth, with worldwide responsibilities for all Human Resources activities.

Previously, Jeremy led the global professional talent acquisition functions for all of Universal Studios and the Universal Music Group businesses. In his role as Corporate Director, Workforce Planning & Strategic Talent Acquisition for Universal Studios, Inc., Jeremy and his team provided leadership for all of the worldwide professional staffing, workforce planning, internal sourcing, college and community organization relations and recruitment, and executive recruitment activities within the Universal organization.

Jeremy previously held positions at Heublein, Inc., The Knott's Organization, and spent several years in human resources, recruitment and talent acquisition with Hyatt Hotels Corporation.

Jeremy holds a Bachelor of Science from California State Polytechnic University (Cal Poly Pomona). As a professional member of the prestigious National Speakers Association (NSA), Jeremy speaks to many audiences on the value of the Talent Acquisition function.

Jeremy is a member of the Institute of Management Consultants-USA (IMC-USA) and the Society for Human Resource Management (SHRM), where he recently served on the national Talent Acquisition Management Special Expertise Panel and the Workforce Planning Standards Workgroup.

Jeremy holds certifications as a Senior Professional in Human Resources (SPHR) from the Human Resources Certification Institute (HRCI), as a Senior Certified Professional (SHRM-SCP) from the Society for Human Resources Management, and as a Certified Management Consultant (CMC) from the Institute of Management Consultants-USA. A native of Southern California, now residing in Long Beach, in addition to his professional affiliations, Jeremy is a member of the Pasadena Tournament of Roses Association. Jeremy may be contacted via email: Jeremy@RecruitCONSULT.net

ACKNOWLEDGEMENTS

Great advice, counsel, criticism, encouragement, and feedback are some of the elements that helped create this book—both in its original first edition and this, the second edition. I would like to thank my team at Riviera Advisors—John Carrozza, Brad Loewen, Ginny Eagle, James Mueller, Dan Kilgore, Sue Pierce and Miranda Horton—for their insights, encouragement, and feedback. I would also like to give thanks to our Riviera Advisors alumni—Diana Meisenhelter, John Vlastelica, Bradley Pritchard and Mary Claire Ryan—for their insights and inspiration while they worked with our team. In 2006, my Riviera Advisors team and I created and launched the Strategic Talent Acquisition Roundtable (STARoundtable) Corporate Talent Acquisition Leadership Academy with the express purpose of delivering high-quality content on how to LEAD recruiting and Talent Acquisition functions rather than how to DO recruiting and staffing. We created great content for the STARoundtable, and some of that content has been incorporated into this book. Thanks again to John, Mary Claire, Diana, and Bradley for their good work on that project.

I especially want to thank the talented current and former Riviera Advisors interns. Thank you to Ray Hailey, Melany Jensen, Chris Stringfellow, Seyka Mejeur, Alyssa Salindong, Regina Kim, Andrew Sandoval, and Crystal Foo. I want to especially thank our 2017-2018 Talent Acquisition Analyst Intern, Miranda Horton for her tremendous work in doing research for this new second edition and for the outstanding proofreading work.

Thanks also goes out to the many Talent Acquisition, Recruiting, Staffing and Human Resources professionals who provided insights into the content of this book (for both the original 2011 first edition and this second edition) and its source material, including Adele Png, Alan Donoghue, Jason Farr, Dr. Cheryl-Marie Hansberger, Christine de la Paz, Vicki Perry, Chelle Wingeleth, Susan Warner, Mike Adamo, Martin Percival, Rodney Moses, Aziz Chowdhury, and Roel Lambrichts. Thanks to the many more of my colleagues, former co-workers, team members, bosses, clients, friends, and family all over the world.

A special thanks goes out to my writing and editorial partners. Thanks to Shayne Lightner, who worked diligently over the last few years to assist me in developing and writing many of the articles and publications I have authored, some of which have been used as source material for the original first edition of this book. Thanks to Thomas A. Hauck for his writing and editorial savvy and publishing expertise on the first edition. A special thanks to Dianne Tennen for her extraordinary writing and editing skills on both the first and second editions. I would also like to thank Maureen Henson, who co-authored a whitepaper on Workforce planning many years ago that has also been adapted for this book.

PREFACE

When I was the head of Talent Acquisition at a large global media company, I noticed our use of third-party search firms was completely inconsistent throughout the company. It was driven by cronyism and individual relationships between the Hiring Managers and external Recruiters.

While attending a conference, I saw a presentation on a "preferred provider relationship" where the Talent Acquisition group used a consultant to help structure the agreement with a third-party search firm. I was reluctant to use a consultant because, after all, wasn't that my job? But after speaking with this particular consultant, I realized he knew more than I did. I also realized that the culture shift I was shooting for was big enough (as were the cost savings) that I needed help. And if it worked, regardless of whether I used a consultant or not, we would all look good.

I lobbied my boss to spend a substantial amount of money to hire the consultant. I met some internal conflict, but I was willing to defend my decision to those voicing their doubts—no matter how loudly they cried. My credibility was at stake, but I believed in the idea, and this was a bet I was willing to take. I had pushed in my entire stack of chips.

My gamble worked. The consultant was worth every penny, and the experience was a highlight of my career. I can actually say that for a time, I changed the culture of a company. I stepped up and made my impact just as other senior leaders in the organization had.

After seeing just how impactful a Talent Acquisition transformation was, I was inspired to help others, and after many years as a consultant, I wrote the first edition of this book to share some of what I had learned.

While I published the first edition many years ago, I still get a lot of feedback that it helped Talent Acquisition leaders think about transformation needed in their own organizations. With these new updates, I hope to re-capture and share what I am so passionate about and provide another way for readers to thrive; whether you are currently leading a Talent Acquisition function, or hope to one day.

Take RecruitCONSULT! Leadership from where it was and fast forward to today; things look very different. It's not simply that things have changed, which is inevitable, it's the speed in which the change has continued to accelerate. Especially for us in Talent Acquisition, which as a function and practice, is faster moving than any other business practice in HR and perhaps all of business. We see this in the way technology has changed, the candidate marketplace has changed, and the way people organize work has changed (just to name a few). I thought it relevant to publish an update of the book to continue to help you, as a strategic Talent Acquisition leader, see the world as it appears today and continue to share my learnings.

The question still is: "When good things happen in Talent Acquisition/ HR within organizations, why is it left to others, like consultants (i.e., me), to write this book?"

Because we as talent acquisition leaders don't always think we're legit. Because we don't have the confidence to let things go. But because our profession needs it, we do need to share what works with other Talent Acquisition professionals and share it in the right way.

For me, one of the wrong ways is when successful HR execs talk about what worked for them as "best practices." Let's get something straight. There are no "best practices". To say something is a "best" practice assumes that what works in one environment will work in all others, which we know isn't true. "Success practices" are those approaches that have worked for one company and may or may not work for another.

I think it's important to communicate your successes—what you're doing that's working. There's some reticence in this area because of the war for talent. But the type of content in this book can't just be left up to the consultants. Time is a rare commodity, and you, the HR/Talent Acquisition professionals, are on the front lines, watching and urging innovation at every turn. Communicating what you're doing can help others.

Those in more established administrative roles, such as marketing, share information because they have confidence and an easy camaraderie that allows them to let things go. We need to have equal confidence in our roles and our profession. We need to stop the negativity and the self-flagellation. We aren't broken and we are legit. At the end of the day, companies and businesses are and always have been about people. Any decent leader will tell you that. Thus, we are the keys to the future. We need to believe that, in our bones, we can let things go and know it will help, not hurt, us. We need to have pride in the HR/ Talent Acquisition profession!

—Jeremy Eskenazi

The RecruitCONSULT! Website

As an owner of this new, second edition of RecruitCONSULT! Leadership, you have access to the RecruitCONSULT.net website and the book owner's password-protected resource page. The resource page has tools, templates, article and other resources you can access and download at any time.

To access the site, visit RecruitCONSULT.net

Click on "Book Owner's Resource Page" and then enter the following password:

2018RC@TopTalent!

(Make sure you remember that the password is case sensitive and to include all punctuation)

INTRODUCTION

Within companies, corporate Talent Acquisition has historically been seen as transactional, administrative, and sometimes less effective than external sources such as third-party search firms and agencies—"headhunters"—in attracting and managing talent.

Over the last 25 years, that has changed immensely because of the professionalization of corporate Talent Acquisition. By the way, what do we call ourselves? There are so many different descriptors we use to define our profession: Recruiting, Staffing, Talent Acquisition, and Employment, just to name a few. For the purposes of this book, I have chosen to use the title "Talent Acquisition" because it is a holistic term that encompasses all that we are responsible for – it's more than filling roles – we are involved in all aspects of movement of talent in, out, up, down, and across an organization. This means that while many people in our profession like to use the term "recruiting" to describe their title or team, recruiting as a function really only means attracting and hiring outside talent into the organization. Clearly we do much more than that.

There have been immense changes in the way the profession seeks talent, for example, through the use of electronic and social media. Way back when, they relied on the passive recruiting methods of placing advertising and waiting for the resumes or CVs to arrive and then administering the assessment of candidates and moving them through the process. Today, many organizations have built sophisticated Talent Acquisition functions that leverage significant technology, tools, and recruiting techniques to hire top talent into their organizations.

However, the role of the leader of these functions has been either slow to change or not sophisticated enough to really add value. Many leaders are placed in their roles simply because they were great Recruiters or individual practitioners. Like promoting a Sales Manager simply because he or she is a great salesperson, this often makes for bad leadership. Just because you may have been great at recruiting doesn't mean you can be great at leading Recruiters.

The job of Talent Acquisition leader has become significantly more complicated with the advent of so many recruiting tools available on the market today—applicant and talent management technology, social media, online databases, analytic tools, online job marketing and job boards, and more—as well as the globalization of many large companies. Leaders are expected to know how to lead a Talent Acquisition function across vast and decentralized global enterprises. Also, organizations expect much more of administrators today; they expect true Talent Acquisition strategists who can really drive competitive value for the organization and win through talent.

In many developed economies of the world, professionals are thought-centric—we no longer *make* things; we *think* things. So talent is even more important to organizations, and the role of the Talent Acquisition leader is critical.

To help move the Talent Management profession forward, this book will discuss the important issues facing our industry, including:

- *Workforce planning* – the concept of strategic workforce planning as a blueprint for future development of Talent Acquisition strategies and organizational structures.

- *Technology* and the speed of change around technology – there are many, many great tools, and as a Talent Acquisition leader, you know it's not a simple plug and play. Any new additions have to integrate well into your existing web of Talent Acquisition tools, and your team and stakeholders have to be onboard and comfortable using them.

- *Analytics* and the need not only to derive the insights that are useful to your business, but the ones that people care about. Is the data you're collecting telling you a useful story and can you translate that story into something meaningful to your business.

- *Metrics* and economics of the internal Talent Acquisition organization. How to fund and pay for the resources for Talent Acquisition and recruiting inside an organization, as well as how to develop and design metrics to measure success and to adjust where necessary.

- *Organizing, leading, and managing* a consultative Talent Acquisition team – how to find recruiting and Talent Acquisition professionals and tips on how to organize the Talent Acquisition function, as well as tips on leading and motivating team members in a consultative Talent Acquisition environment.

- *Leading a proactive Talent Acquisition function* that actually recruits using the RecruitCONSULT! philosophy. This means recruiting (attracting and finding) top talent to an organization. There are so many recruiting teams that passively post and pray. Active recruiting is actively seeking out candidates by leveraging resume/CV databases, performing web search, engaging social networks, using good old-fashioned direct sourcing/cold calling, and pursuing other headhunting activities.

- *Using RPO* in the right ways – never give up your 'mojo'. There should be a strategy focused on keeping the most important work at the core, and thoughtfully using outsourcing partners to scale and supplement your operation quickly. Getting Talent Acquisition off the books may make your accounting team happy, but it will end up costing you more in the end.

- *Organizational politics* for the Talent Acquisition leader—the reality of the role of a corporate Talent Acquisition leader in what may be the most difficult part of the job; navigating organizational politics.

- *The power of relationships* inside and outside the organization—a discussion on the power of relationships as a key element of success for corporate Talent Acquisition leaders (both internally as well as externally) as well as dealing with third-party resources (such as search firms and agencies), and other HR teams.

- *Change management*—a discussion on managing and leading through change in a corporate Talent Acquisition environment.

- *Leading global teams, but keeping recruiting local* —how leaders leverage their resources in a global environment, and some of the unique issues in recruiting across a global footprint.

- *How your approach as a leader* and your ability to tell the story of the team can directly impact your success.

THE RecruitCONSULT! TALENT ACQUISITION ORGANIZATION MATURITY MODEL

Before we begin our journey, I would like to share and discuss the Recruit-CONSULT! Talent Acquisition Organization Maturity Model, which charts the four general stages of development of an organization's Talent Acquisition function. I will show the costs of the earlier stages and the increasing benefits as the organization moves from Stage I which is hit-or-miss decentralized recruiting – to Stage IV, which is planned and profitable strategic recruiting.

Stage I: Decentralized Recruiting. The most inefficient operational model. Individuals and business units recruit independently, following a generic process that is loosely defined and without structure. There is a reliance on passive recruiting (where we are passive and the candidates are active).

Stage II: Internal Recruiters Hired. Experienced Recruiters are brought on board, but they have little experience with our business and culture. Because of a lack of structure, Recruiters are unable to tighten the process from the bottom up. Executives who could provide guidance do not fully understand or appreciate the recruitment process. Technology is used but not leveraged fully. There is continued reliance on passive recruiting.

Stage III: Process Improvement Initiatives. Strong executive leadership results in movement toward professionalization and investment. Customer process flows are designed, documented, and communicated. Internal education and training is put into place. Recruiters analyze current and future states and gap analysis, and they benchmark metrics. Technology is stable and used effectively throughout the organization. Secure relationships are created with vendors, university recruiting, and others. Active recruiting is initiated (we actively seek candidates, who themselves may be passive).

Stage IV: Strategic Staffing. This is where every organization needs to be. Top-down participation is recognized and rewarded. Bottom-line results are apparent in disciplined and iterative planning cycles. There are both strategic, cost-effective sourcing and end-to-end linkages with related HR functions (recruit, grow, retain). There is regular tracking and reporting against goals and service level agreements (SLAs). Information feedback loops and evolutionary process improvement keep the program moving forward. A mix of active and passive recruiting maximizes return on investment.

In the chart below, I discuss the *transition enablers* with each stage that need to be in place for the organization to move up from its current stage to the next and ultimately to Stage IV: Strategic Talent Acquisition.

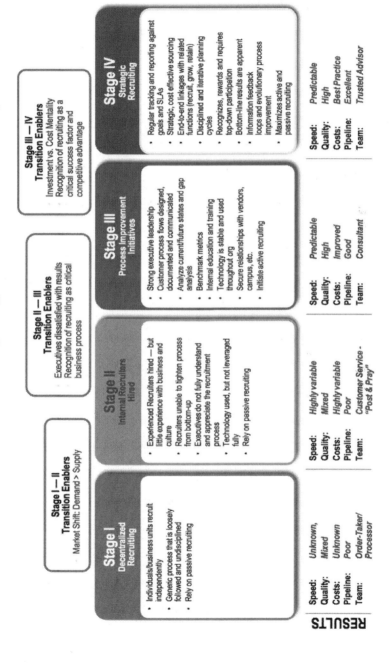

RecruitCONSULT! Staffing Organization Maturity Model

Stage I — II Transition Enablers
Market Shift: Demand > Supply

Stage II — III Transition Enablers
Executives dissatisfied with results
Recognition of recruiting as critical business process

Stage III — IV Transition Enablers
Investment vs. Cost Mentality
Recognition of recruiting as a critical success factor and competitive advantage

Stage I
Decentralized Recruiting

- Individuals/business units recruit independently
- Generic process that is loosely followed and undisciplined
- Rely on passive recruiting

Speed: Unknown,
Quality: Mixed
Costs: Unknown
Pipeline: Poor
Team: Order-Taker/ Processor

Stage II
Internal Recruiters Hired

- Experienced Recruiters hired — but little experience with business and culture
- Recruiters unable to tighten process from bottom-up
- Executives do not fully understand and appreciate the recruitment process
- Technology used, but not leveraged fully
- Rely on passive recruiting

Speed: Highly variable
Quality: Mixed
Costs: Highly variable
Pipeline: Poor
Team: Customer Service - "Post & Pray"

Stage III
Process Improvement Initiatives

- Strong executive leadership
- Customer process flows designed, documented and communicated
- Analyze current/future states and gap analysis
- Benchmark metrics
- Internal education and training
- Technology is stable and used throughout org
- Secure relationships with vendors, campus, etc.
- Initiate active recruiting

Speed: Predictable
Quality: High
Costs: Improved
Pipeline: Good
Team: Consultant

Stage IV
Strategic Recruiting

- Regular tracking and reporting against goals and SLAs
- Strategic, cost effective sourcing
- End-to-end linkages with related functions (recruit, grow, retain)
- Disciplined and iterative planning cycles
- Recognizes, rewards and requires top-down participation
- Bottom-line results are apparent
- Information feedback loops and evolutionary process improvement
- Maximizes active and passive recruiting

Speed: Predictable
Quality: High
Costs: Best Practice
Pipeline: Excellent
Team: Trusted Advisor

RESULTS

I bring these concepts together in a practical, down-to-earth field guide that incorporates the stories and authentically direct language style that I have used in my many articles. You can check some of these out, as well as other helpful resources at www.recruitconsult.net click on the Book Owners Resource Site button and use the password: 2018RC-TopTalent! (Make sure you remember that the password is case sensitive and to include all punctuation) to unlock additional content. As a new or experienced Talent Acquisition leader, you can leverage these concepts and practices immediately in your organization.

CHAPTER 1: WORKFORCE PLANNING

If professionals in the Talent Acquisition profession could predict what positions, roles, functions, and skills would be needed by organizations in the future, could they be more successful? The answer is *absolutely.*

Why then do many Talent Acquisition professionals feel as if they are always operating in a reactive mode? Usually the reason is that true workforce planning is not being accomplished *inside* the organization.

What is workforce planning, you may be asking. It is the process of assessing workforce content and composition to respond to future business needs. It is the key to strategic Talent Acquisition.

Simplified, workforce planning is a systematic process to analyze the gap between what organizational talent a business has and what it needs in the future. Often workforce planning adds an additional important component: an assessment and plan for addressing the gaps that were identified.

Organizational success depends on having the right employees, with the right competencies, at the right time. Workforce planning provides managers the means of identifying the competencies workers need in the present and in the future and then selecting and developing workers with those competencies.

Instead of starting over each time they get a requisition or a request to fill a job, Talent Acquisition professionals using workforce planning will have already developed plans and begun sourcing to fill their needs.

Some components of workforce planning, such as workforce demographics, retirement projections, and succession planning, are familiar to managers. Workforce planning provides focus to these components and more refined information on changes to anticipate, the competencies that retirements and other uncontrollable actions will take from the workforce, and fill key positions. This in turn allows managers to plan replacements and changes in workforce competencies.

To most Talent Acquisition professionals, this whole idea sounds great, but the reality is that many will question why a recruiting professional should spend time and energy on developing plans when the common view is that recruiting is *reactive*. If change is constant in our world, why bother making long-range recruitment plans?

BENEFITS OF WORKFORCE PLANNING

The 'why' of workforce planning is grounded in the benefits to managers and the planning and strategy cycles of the business as a whole. Workforce planning provides managers with a strategy for making Human Resource decisions. It allows them to *anticipate* change rather than being surprised by events and to provide strategic methods for addressing present and anticipated workforce issues.

Experience has taught us that the costs associated with planning are more than offset by the savings incurred from hiring the best possible person for a position. The resulting benefits of lower employee turnover, higher productivity, and the creation of an effective internal succession pipeline far outweigh the initial investment. Here are a few of the benefits of workforce planning:

- It lowers the cost of unplanned recruiting and boosts a company's profitability through improved productivity.

- Shifts in the labor market make planning for workforce needs essential; organizations can no longer afford to accept short-term solutions and then be forced to respond when conditions change.

- The labor pool does not dynamically expand in direct correlation to most companies' talent needs. For example, while there may be a large number of workers who have been affected by layoffs, organizations may be seeking workers with specific skills that are not readily available.

- Companies in a growth mode are increasingly challenged to acquire critical talent required to achieve business objectives over the long-term but with specific milestones in the short term.

- Workforce planning enables *relationship* recruitment rather than *incident* recruitment. That is, you can understand what specific types of people, competencies, and skills you will need in the future and can develop relationships with sources of that talent well before you have to fill a role.

- HR and Talent Acquisition professionals are viewed more as strategic business partners by the businesses they support.

- Shifting from a short-term transactional mode to a consultative model provides greater breadth and depth of Talent Acquisition management and long-term improvement to an organization's bottom line.

- New business developments and changes are more easily incorporated, and priorities are adjusted on the basis of collaboration with the business.

As a Talent Acquisition professional, if you lead or participate in a workforce planning initiative, you will be placed squarely into the strategic business planning process for your organization. You can align your daily recruiting tasks to the strategy the business will be using (learned through your workforce planning). For Talent Acquisition professionals, as well as generalist HR professionals who have responsibilities for recruiting, I have identified a few great reasons to implement workforce planning.

ANALYTICAL WORKFORCE PLANNING

Many Talent Acquisition professionals like the idea of workforce planning, but often it gets pushed aside in favor of more reactive work (like filling requisitions). Few really understand how to "do" workforce planning.

Whole books have been written on workforce planning. This chapter is solely meant as an introduction to the concept. Hopefully it will create interest and curiosity within your own organization to learn more.

The analytic workforce planning process is really a process of coordination. Often the single most daunting task is getting the data necessary to analyze the workforce. To gather the data, the solution is straightforward: you interview managers of individual workgroups inside your organization, and then you consolidate and analyze that data. You'll create a set of standard questions to ask each manager.

Here are a few key components in workforce planning:

Current Workforce Supply Assessment. Take a look at the competencies of the organization's current employees to achieve business objectives.

Future Workforce Supply Assessment. Review your current supply and add in any known variables (prior demand, known openings, attrition, performance review data) and unknown variables using your past experience, or industry trends (transfers, terminations, competitive factors).

Demand Forecast. Determine what competencies or employees will be required to achieve business objectives for a specified time in the future.

Gap Review. The gap is a comparison of current and future supply to demand forecasts. Gaps can be filled by transfers, external talent acquisitions, outsourcing, or contracting.

Here are some specific actions you should take if you are going to lead a workforce planning effort:

Planning

Take a look at your organization and break it into chunks. Look at your organizational structure, go down to the most basic workgroup level (such as division, department, or team), and determine who the leaders are. You'll then need to create a list of standard questions to ask them about their business and their workgroup. Here are some examples of questions to ask:

- What are the key business goals and objectives for the next year? We used to be able to ask for longer, but that is no longer a viable approach.

- What is our competitive environment like, and how will it impact your ability to meet these goals and objectives?

- What are the critical processes that are needed to meet those goals?

- What are the key success factors for achieving future outcomes?

- What are the key work activities associated with these success factors?

- What are the barriers to optimal performance of the work activities?

- What talent pools can affect those barriers?

- What features of your current talent pool may impact your ability to achieve success in the future?

- What people capabilities are needed to deliver on those critical processes?

- What are the most critical people issues (including availability of the skills you need and the cost of these skills) you currently face?

- What do you think the most critical people issues will be in six months to one year?

- Which positions and capabilities are most critical to your business?

Prepare Workgroup Leaders

Make sure you prepare the managers you'll be interviewing. You may want to call, visit, or send an e-mail and let them know the purpose of the interview you'll be having with them. Perhaps you can even send them some of the sample questions you'll be asking them in your interview. You will also want to gather a list of all the employees in each workgroup and bring that to your interview with each workgroup manager.

Conduct Workgroup Leader Interviews

During your interview you'll want to clearly identify the future business state for the workgroup: what will need to be done in the workgroup in the next six to eighteen months (or longer)? What are the goals and objectives of the workgroup, and more importantly, what skills and competencies will be required of the team? You will then review each of the current employees and assess them based on the skills and competencies needed in the future. This should be a quick assessment. You will then discuss the perceived gaps in the business needs and the competencies of the current workgroup.

Analyze Outcomes and Develop the Demand Analysis

After you gather all of the information from the interviews, you'll want to track what you learned on a simple spreadsheet that will identify what your workgroups told you about what they have, what they will need in the future, and what their future demand requirements will be for talent.

Gap Analysis

You can then review the information you have learned from the exercise and create your assumptions. You can make a good guesstimate of what types of positions, people, and competencies will be needed in the future.

Building Plans

Now you will be able to plan on how gaps will be addressed. Will you "build or buy"—will you develop talent internally or go out and attract new talent with the right skills and competencies you need? You'll now want to plan your execution of the Talent Acquisition plans and align the resources you will need.

TRANSLATING DATA INTO STRATEGY

Once you have accomplished the action steps of planning, working with your leadership teams, and analyzing the supply/demand of your talent needs and pools, what are your next steps?

The data gathered from your leadership interviews should provide you with the strategic direction of the business moving forward. Don't worry, we'll get deep into how to approach data gathering through tools and technology, analysis, and measurement in coming chapters. Questions that should be answered during these discussions include:

- What is the revenue growth potential? Will this translate into additions to staff or will the current human capital resources be sufficient in current numbers to support this growth strategy?

- How will competitors react to your Talent Acquisition needs and how will you be able to differentiate your employment brand succinctly enough to attract the right mix and caliber of talent to meet this need?

- Where can talent be developed from in-house (bench strength) and when will it be necessary to seek such talent and skills from the external environment? What will be the timing of each? It's important to understand the current demographics of the in-house workforce in terms of turnover, projected retirements, and skill sets and competencies both today and in the future to meet these business demands. It's also important to note what the full-time/part-time/contractor mix is in terms of an effective Talent Acquisition model.

- Where are the most lucrative yet cost-effective sources for the talent/competencies that will be required? Timing and competitive pressures here need to be considered.

- What, if any, labor contracts or agreements—whether through labor union(s) or some other entity—need to be taken into account regarding future workforce planning?

The labor market, both internally and externally, should be reviewed and carefully correlated with the business demands so that the talent pool availability can be adequately assessed. Understanding the components and drivers of the talent pool are critical. Some key questions that will need to be addressed include:

- Will the *talent* be readily available, or will competition for the skill sets needed be intense?

- What will *motivate* such a talent pool to join your company or even the industry?

- Are the *skills (skills are the things that top talent brings to your organiza-*

tion) needed readily available, or will there need to be an investment of training and development?

Once you have mapped the business needs to the talent pool analysis you can then begin to build Talent Acquisition plans that include Talent Procurement strategies. It is also critical to build in measures of effectiveness for each source that is used to attract the needed talent. These sources can include print or electronic advertising, digital and social networks, recruitment events, employee referrals, image advertising, college and universities, trade and industry sources, or even customer referrals of available talent.

Contract and Temporary Labor

One source that should not be overlooked is the contract or temporary ("contingent") labor pool that can be an effective feeder into the regular work force. Frequently this temporary labor pool can be a viable source of talent "audition"—that is, a way for both the employee and employer to determine whether or not the employment experience is a good fit for either party. The trend toward a master/vendor agreement where there is a sole source master provider (with subcontractors managed by the master vendor) for contingent Talent Acquisition allows a company to realize cost savings. At the same time, they will be able to explore the labor market potential through the outsourced vendor who bears much of the employment burden.

Timelines and Projections

On a spreadsheet where you have captured the organization's needs based on your leadership interviews and analysis of the current and future workforce, you will need to add the talent pool projections and sourcing strategies with appropriate measures incorporated at every stage of execution. It is also important that the appropriate timelines be incorporated both on a short and long-term projection.

Many organizations that choose analytic workforce planning are highly structured, organized, and numbers driven. The types of organizations that I have seen do the highly analytical workforce planning process really well typically have many of the same types of employees and have solid historical business patterns. For example, airlines know how many flight crews they need and what the business historically was on any given day or season. As a result, they can predict demand effectively. They also have many of the same types of employees (flight attendants, pilots, reservation agents). Other types of organizations that can do this perhaps more effectively than others include utility companies, hotels, cruise lines, theme parks, and retail stores. However, not all organizations want or need this highly structured process. They can accomplish what I call "Anecdotal Workforce Planning."

Instead of a long-term strategy developed and published at the executive level, Anecdotal Workforce Planning is more fluid and responds to changing conditions. For this approach to work, the keys are communication and simplicity.

- It's all about the dialogue. Break down Hiring Managers into work units and ask for estimates, hiring plans, budget plans, and other planning tools to be prioritized with managers.

- Keep it simple. Still use a standardized questionnaire as I have already discussed. Workforce planning must be used to drive organizational and sourcing design. Design a template to ask the same questions of managers and conduct interviews. Design a Talent Acquisition strategy around the prioritization grid, and then plot the positions/ jobs. Review the prioritization grid with the business leaders and Hiring Managers. Execute using internal and external resources as planned. Review and repeat this process on a regular basis to recalibrate (quarterly is suggested).

Prioritization Grid Example

DEVELOPING TALENT ACQUISITION STRATEGIES

Now that you understand workforce planning and can map out your own plans using the prioritization grid, a well-developed game plan should be formed. This is what I refer to as a Talent Acquisition strategy. The purpose of this strategy is to meet the hiring goals of an organization using business objectives gathered during your workforce planning. You will then come to an agreement that the plan is in fact what the organization needs. By reaching this agreement with business leaders, you have established a map that will provide direction to your team and help drive the organization proactively forward, both from a cost and a tactical perspective. The Talent Acquisition strategy can also act as the basis for any business cases you may need to develop in order to secure the resources you will need to make the right hires.

No two strategies will be identical, but I've come to see a few execution levels that have been effective. The level at which you devise your Talent Acquisition plan will depend on a number of factors unique to your work environment and needs. These considerations are:

- Timelines of the hires required.

- Additional information required in order to meet business needs.

- Reputation and credibility of the Talent Acquisition team.

- How information and progress will be shared and communicated with leaders.

With this information and understanding of the more immediate needs you can choose from three levels of Talent Acquisition strategies: organization, function, or job. If the *organization-wide* Talent Acquisition strategy is going to be the best fit, it should encompass a *minimum* of six months and *maximum* of eighteen months. We used to be able to go up to three years, but given the speed of change, Talent Acquisition is changing and/or evolving very quickly, you can see how the time investment too far out is futile. However, with the change-filled times we are in, eighteen months may be as far out as you can plan and still be realistic about execution. This strategy is often driven by the senior Talent Acquisition leader but could be developed by anyone in HR. The objective is to ensure that both replacement and new-hire hiring needs are based on forecasted numbers across organizational units and job families. Keep in mind your sourcing channels when reviewing Talent Acquisition at the organization level. This could include social media, university recruiting, and employer branding initiatives.

When working at this level it will also be important to promote your team and its services to your business leaders. Many companies do have the internal talent to work with agency swiftness and professionalism, and one way to demonstrate this is through the development of a charter. The charter should outline the Talent Acquisition principles and philosophies of the team to provide context to Hiring Managers when working on hard-to-fill or critical priority hires. Now the business will better understand why you may request four interviews for some roles and how their patience and faith in the process will yield the best-fit candidates the team needs.

Taking the scope down a level, you may want to work on a *functional* Talent Acquisition strategy (or organizational unit). By using your workforce plans and leveraging the relationships formed when deriving your Talent Acquisition strategy, this level is driven by a Talent Acquisition leader in partnership with the department heads, Hiring Managers, and HR team within a department. There will be very specific resources provided to execute the final plans, which will often involve an element of prioritization. The last ingredient recommended for success at the functional level (but really should be considered regardless) is communication. Being transparent, open, and clear about what you are working on and the progress and status of hires-to-plan will only add to the confidence in the Talent Acquisition strategy; try to develop or use existing mechanisms to deliver updates, be it weekly or monthly.

The most micro-level approach is the *job* Talent Acquisition strategy (or individual requisition). At this detailed level you are often looking for a specific set of skills and will need to employ a different strategy than at the organizational or functional level. The strategy for job Talent Acquisition is unique as it requires consideration for critical skills, where these skills are in the market, and what the "carrot" is for this type of candidate. Developing an action plan is a good idea to help keep focus as you source, evaluate, and sell these candidates to Hiring Managers. Keeping to your action plan will help with the time-to-fill guideline from your charter. While a Talent Acquisition leader should have an overview of job Talent Acquisition strategies, at this level it is often developed and executed by the Recruiter in partnership with the Hiring Manager (or HR support partner depending on the support model of the organization). Information and updates should be shared regularly, especially once you get into selling the front running candidates.

These three areas seem pretty straightforward in theory, but in the middle of the action you may need additional guidance before deciding which level will be most beneficial. Type of candidate, resourcing, and measurement are often good indicators of which Talent Acquisition strategy you will want to proceed with.

It can be a challenge to make the time to create a Talent Acquisition strategy, but with the right level, the plan will maximize your continued success.

Here are just a few of the many benefits you will realize if you use a Talent Acquisition strategy. Once you have been through this process a few times, it will become second nature.

Outcome	Hiring activity plan	Sourcing strategy	Process alignment to hiring goals	Communication plan
	Show detailed goals and progress for interviews	Source-of-hire targets for each job/category (primary and secondary)	Resource alignment as process established	Identified ownership of updates and schedules
	Map offer presentations and acceptances	Update sourcing strategy to meet role needs	Establish an SLA between the recruiter and hiring manager	Milestone planning and recognition
	Calendar of start dates	Exposure to new areas for potential future sourcing	Focus on efficiency and repeatable process	Matrix of which stakeholders require updates to keep all informed at the right times
	Access to detailed information by category and priority roles	Bring more strategy to the role and move towards a consultative model	Ease of training and onboarding for new staffing team members	Increased credibility and customer-focused staffing

CASE STUDIES

Here's how workforce planning has been implemented in three real organizations.

Company X is a large, U.S.-based, billion-dollar company involved in design, manufacturing, and marketing of specialized medical devices with approximately 80,000 employees worldwide. It was growing by about 5% – 7% per year in sales when it implemented a workforce planning process.

The company decided it needed to better understand where to leverage the limited resources it had to spend on Talent Acquisition costs. After an exhaustive review using some of the same tools described within this book, the company identified that the key strategic areas for the company's future success were Research & Development Engineering and Manufacturing Engineering. Although other parts of the organization were very important (such as sales, marketing, and support functions), these two areas were most critical.

Instead of building a Talent Acquisition function to support all areas of the organization, this company determined they would build a Talent Acquisition strategy that would solely focus on these two critical areas and outsource the rest. Specifically, this company would build a highly specialized Talent Acquisition team that would focus only on building deep expertise in Research & Development Engineering and Manufacturing Engineering.

The company wisely chose to invest in building the right talent for the team with Talent Acquisition professionals who had solid expertise in developing and maintaining relationships with this specialized pool of talent.

The remaining recruiting needs of the organization were managed by a small group of Project Management-oriented Talent Acquisition professionals who managed vendor relationships with search, research, and other outsourced recruiting professionals. The sole focus of the company's investment was in the critical functions.

Company X's results have been excellent. Since building the specialized Talent Acquisition function, the time it takes to fill the most critical roles in the company is very low. This is because the organization is consistently recruiting and building/maintaining relationships with prospective candidates at all times in the critical functions. They have a solid pipeline of talent in the areas they know they'll need in the future. In addition, manager and candidate satisfaction levels are higher than in the past.

Company X's experience shows that even with limited budgets organizations can shift their focus and spending to cover the most critical areas of need rather than try to do it all.

Company Y, a five-billion-dollar global manufacturer and marketer of industrial and consumer goods, decided it wanted to consolidate all of its internal and external recruiting processes into a single "shared service" environment. There was significant duplication in the amount of work each of the many separate business units and locations conducted in this area, and the company determined that by consolidating these functions it could significantly improve service and lower costs. In order to do this effectively, the company had to go through a very significant workforce planning process to determine how they would build this new consolidated Talent Acquisition organization. The company recognized that if they did not know what the future would look like in the next few years they could not effectively design and build a more streamlined Talent Acquisition operation.

Company Y took on the process of workforce planning in a very structured way. They developed a simple workgroup leader interview template and then did a train-the-trainer session for its HR leaders. The HR leaders went out into the businesses and conducted many interviews across the organization. The result was significant trend data from hundreds of managers leading workgroups on talent needs, gaps, and issues. It also provided an anecdotal workforce future forecast. This data was consolidated and provided the blueprint for the new Talent Acquisition organization.

The company was able to use the workforce planning data to drive the design of the Talent Acquisition function (including how many Recruiters it needed, how much it would outsource/insource, and how much internal development was necessary on the current employee population). With the data in hand, Company Y built its new Talent Acquisition function with much more rigor and data-driven decisions and that new function has been successfully operating for several years. An additional benefit of the workforce planning exercise was that the organization development team now also had access to the workforce planning document and has been able to use it in its own development of curriculum, training, and other developmental decisions.

Company Z – A pharmaceutical company I once worked with was looking at their current model, which was fully outsourced to an RPO (Recruitment Process Outsourcing company). After a long intensive assessment on cost, quality, time, and metrics, they decided they wanted to re-insource the function. We started with conducting a quick workforce planning process in which they asked all the HR Generalists and Talent Acquisition team members that supported individual business units about their needs. We invested time with ad hoc business leaders, not the most senior person, the individual Hiring Managers. We asked things like, how many people you will hire in next two years, where are they located, what skills they will need. With this anecdotal information obtained from simple dialogue, they worked with ballpark numbers. The Talent Acquisition and HR Generalist teams used a spreadsheet and plotted the data from their five dozen meetings or so, and created a 2x2 box grid (from earlier in the chapter). By using this Prioritization Grid it showed us how many jobs and job titles were needed by prioritized title. The high uniqueness, low priority we were seeing were outsourced to agencies. The work to create a portfolio and get the agencies on board which would specialize in those jobs and be established to find these roles was a deliberate and strategic move. For low uniqueness and less high-priority jobs, we decided to use temp-regular hires and allow the temporary roles to convert into full time employees, or outsource totally. These were functions like security, mailroom, cafeteria staff, and not have these as our employees and we used a managed service provider for administrative roles. Jobs on one side of the grid even helped them to build a new Talent Acquisition team. Prior to this exercise, the company was paying the RPO to do all these things at a very high price. After the assessment, we knew which jobs were needed, where they would be, how hard they would be to fill and how prioritize. We were also able to better set up the Talent Acquisition team including the knowledge of how to build the team, how many Recruiters, Sourcers, and Coordinators we would need. The Workforce Planning process, while it might seem daunting, can really be focused on asking questions in consistent way to influence how you build the team.

CONCULSION

Using the information you gathered through the workforce planning process you will be able to develop a clear sense of the people needs of the organization today, and in the future. And by taking the time to collect it, you will have built a relationship with the business that makes you much more of a strategic partner rather than a HR executor. Today's Talent Acquisition leader has to be able to empower their team to find the right skills for the future and attract the talent needed. The information in a workforce plan can then lead you to build broad sourcing and other Talent Acquisition programs that address the future needs of the organization while allowing your team to focus on the execution of individual searches. It will also allow you to better assess your diversity needs, which become more and more important. We'll talk more about that in future chapters, as diversity will continue to be increasingly important to your success as a business. Workforce planning is your pathway to the future, and with that, we should now talk about the available resources to influence your data gathering.

CHAPTER 2: TALENT ACQUISITION TOOLS AND TECHNOLOGY

In the last chapter, we talked about the need to have a great plan in order to develop a clear sense of the people needs in your organization. Let's assume you're now confident in your workforce plan. You've met with your Hiring Managers, business leaders, and HR partners, and you've shown them how individual talent will be brought into the organization to meet their needs today and tomorrow. Having the right tools and technology is critical in getting you to this step. I'll spend this chapter sharing some of the tools of our trade and the applications available to us. In the next chapter, we'll get into how to best analyze and interpret that data, followed by another chapter on metrics. As you can see, understanding how to collect information, then be able to use it to the advantage of your organization is an important way to be able to show how your team achieves higher quality Talent Acquisition better, faster, and cheaper for success today and tomorrow.

It's clear that a RecruitCONSULT! leader will use a mix of tools and technology to not only optimize their team, reducing time and manual processes, but to gather data. Imagine what would happen if resources on your team had to spend time scanning resumes into a centralized portal, or someone had to search through paper resumes for key skill sets. Your team would be lost in the administrative abyss and you would not have time to create strategic partnerships. The part that can be daunting is when you start to learn about ongoing development of super tools, smart machines, and predictive analytics. With a strategy in place, these tools can greatly enhance the accuracy of the story you want to tell to your Hiring Managers. Without a strategy, administering these tools has the potential to create more noise.

Individuals who become Recruiters *do not* want to spend their days pushing paper. You likely *do not* want to spend your day pushing paper. It's likely you'll have to do some of it, so with the right choices and mix, you can minimize the pain for your entire team.

TOOLS AND TECH USES FOR TALENT ACQUISITION

Tools and technology are great ways to help you achieve a strategy. They provide an executional path to help you speed your processes up. It helps a Recruiter do their day-to-day job instead of doing things manually. Tools create mountains of data that can be organized articulately, easily searched, and stored centrally. This data helps you form solid answers to the questions your clients have about their Talent Acquisition needs, and allows you to proactively move the business into the future.

Here are some technologies that can really help:

- **Cloud-based documentation systems** can be used for a variety of business uses. From a general perspective, they allow for a reduction of approximately 10,000 sheets of paper per year if your numbers are conservative. By reducing paper, you also reduce paperwork. In Talent Acquisition tech, you can use tools that enable e-signatures or give access to online calendars which make scheduling logistics much easier. Paperwork is quicker, and scheduling is automated without a lot of back and forth to finalize.

- **Candidate Relationship Management (CRM)** can help Talent Acquisition much in the same way it does sales. You can share notes, track candidates and a plethora of details they provide through your ATS. You can develop and nurture leads and document your interactions with candidates, as well as balance coverage on your team should the lead Recruiter on a requisition be out of pocket for any amount of time. Online campaigns and leads through these types of events can be tracked, and data will be available at your fingertips – or through an easily created report.

- **Artificial Intelligence (AI)** was scary when it first came out in movies with robots out-smarting humans – this is different. First, I'd like to clarify that the impact of AI on jobs has not been negative overall. Yes, there may be individuals who've had parts of their role replaced by an intelligent system; however, multiple studies have shown growth of hundreds of thousands of human jobs created with the implementation of AI. Like all tools, the purpose of using AI is to improve productivity by reducing repetitive, predictable work. As we can all attest from experience, that often doesn't accurately describe much of a Talent Acquisition professionals' role.

There are two more popular forms of AI that support Talent Acquisition functions. *Open AI* is a more high-end, sleek, futuristic source of intelligence. It has significant capabilities and continues to learn as it's used. *Programmatic AI* is generally supporting the back-end processes and it handles specific tasks or process driven elements of the Talent Acquisition cycle.

Some of the tasks AI can take over include: mining resumes and performing an initial scrub of candidates in an ATS who do not meet the minimum criteria, scheduling interviews, or kicking off a background screening process and managing prompts to complete. When it comes to interviewing, AI can help with scoring video interviews, evaluating any gamified programs used for pre-engagement, and recommend the best candidate based on set criteria.

While it lacks in human warmth, an AI tool can be as powerful as you, the implementer, make it. Part of the success of machine learning is in its ability to predict, or find patterns that you tell it to look for. The fewer the details, or learnings you give the system, the less it will be able to find information that you would find helpful through resumes, social media profiles, Hiring Manager preferences from the ATS, and performance ratings of high performers. Keep in mind that the system grows in a cumulative manner.

Remember, AI is not perfect. It can help reduce errors in repeatable functions, but can also have prejudices that can come from design flaws, or a human telling it that one piece of data is accurate when it is not. Industry leaders have predicted that AI recruiting software and technology is merely an assistant to the recruiting process and will never fully take over the role of a Recruiter.[1] With this in mind, I strongly suggest that you stress this to your team as they are first exposed to AI tools. It will reduce anxiety, and hopefully promote the curiosity and alignment of thought that will help them get the most value from this type of tool.

- **Chatbots** are a part of AI, but as they also standalone from a Talent Acquisition perspective, I'll approach this as a subcategory. A chatbot is a computer program designed to simulate conversation with human users, especially over the Internet. You may have experienced them on retail websites, where some early adopters have implemented them to

---

1   Noel Webb, co-founder of a Canadian-based AI Recruiting tool from http:// theundercoverrecruiter.com/recruiters-ai-work-together/

help shoppers chose a brand of jeans based on their last favorite pair, or suggest a pair of shoes that are often purchased with a particular style of blazer. Chatbots can help with many of the things that AI can do, like scheduling, and reviewing resumes in an ATS, but they can also be candidate facing with personas that are an extension of your employer brand. Examples of this could look like answering basic questions on your careers webpage, or scheduling the candidate's interview in real time. There are some downsides to using chatbots as they have been described here. For example, in any newly developing technology change—there are some people who will be offended by engaging with a chatbot rather than a real person. The more familiar and "user friendly" employers can make their chatbots, the better.

Ultimately, chatbots are able to build candidate profiles because they are able to 'listen' to conversations between candidates and the software, and provide information to build and assess said candidate. From a candidate experience perspective, chatbots have the ability to keep in touch with candidates, keeping them warm, and staying engaged through specific touch points or intervals. This diagram shows you what the process of using a chatbot might look like from the candidate's perspective.[2]

Chatbot Process Flow

2   *Chatbots, AI, Machine Learning, and Recruiting*, Ryan Leary, Recruiting Daily June 23, 2017 http://recruiting daily.com/chatbots-ai-machine-learning-recruiting

- **Applicant Tracking System (ATS)** is a software application that enables the electronic handling of Talent Acquisition needs. Inside the organization, Recruiters can reduce time to contact candidates by using search tools to find the closest fit, instead of reading hundreds, and sometimes thousands, of resumes. While there are open source and free software available, most companies will invest in a license agreement that comes with more features. When the job application process went digital several years ago, it enabled companies to get hundreds of applications in a very short amount of time. This tool helps your team store, rank, route to Hiring Managers, schedule interviews, manage a talent pool, and takes them through paperwork and onboarding. It is the Project Management system that can manage complexities and volume at the same time.

  A recent study[3] focused on the elevation and promotion of a quality candidate experience. It showed that 88% of candidates who had a good experience applying for a job left feeling positive about the employer. This is even when they didn't get the job. One criteria that had a major impact was the quality of the application process.

- **Reference checking/background investigation technologies** are an extremely important part of the hiring process. They can also be long and tedious. Tools for reference and background investigation today have become a lucrative add-on service for many Recruitment Process Outsourcing (RPO) firms. What the tools can do for your team include; automating the process to prompt candidates to kick off the screening, complete most of the requirements online through online signatures, and can act as a project manager for Recruiters. You can update your Hiring Managers quickly by seeing which elements of a background screen are outstanding, and set up alerts for time delays that are outside of your usual scope. Keeping all records digital are also helpful in any future investigations, and understanding if certain findings on the screen result in any future success, or early indicators of a lack of cultural fit.

- **Screening and Assessment technologies** are important indicators for candidate success in the workplace and can reduce the time Recruiters spend on unsuitable candidates – even if they look good on paper. By using existing data, companies can look at several factors to deter-

---

3   Workday Recruiting : Will It Disrupt The Talent Acquisition Software Market?, Josh Bersin, May 6, 2014 https://www.forbes.com/sites/joshbersin/2014/05/06/workday-recruiting-will-it-disrupt-the-talent-acquisition-software-market/#63df25d77681

mine and predict possible business outcomes by looking for specific skill sets or qualities. Nearly 70% of companies report using[4] some sort of pre-employment screening with a goal of assessing validity and reliability of the type of candidate. Companies have been using pre-employment testing earlier on in the recruiting process because it helps to weed out the candidates who do not match the criteria quicker. Testing of applicants can get expensive, which is why there are programs where organizations can pay for "unlimited testing on a subscription basis, as opposed to paying per test." The types of assessments can include measuring for Emotional Intelligence, The Workplace Big Five personality model, The Predictive Index, DiSC profiling, and Clifton's Strength Finder to name a few.

- **Sourcing** has been greatly enhanced by technology. From branding exercises on social media, to talent communities and group discussions within professional associations, to paid ads within social recruiting tools themselves, it has been transformative. It's not just the ability to find talent where they are, it's also about integrating these sources into your other tools to get your ATS to be as comprehensive as possible. Think about sourcing events of the past – for example a job fair at a campus. It's not to say those don't happen anymore, but university recruiting can now be done just as effectively with the use of a computer and the right tools. Employee referral programs are another way technology has helped with sourcing. You can now link referrals to high performing talent much sooner, you can also find affiliations, alumni associations, and better track the source of employees who do well within their first year once hired.

  Think of your campaign management with the use of technology. Email campaigns, tools for mobile communication and new channels to more quickly connect with talent have all been enabled through sourcing tools and technology.

- **Using Social Networks** to make your team more efficient can go either way. Generally I don't recommend using Facebook to recruit candidates, however as a 'push' mechanism of getting information out to specific audiences, it can be useful. It has not shown to be effective from a 'pull' perspective in drawing in candidates as in many markets it is strictly a personal social media tool. While I have seen some companies use Facebook to source, I do warn you that in my experience,

4   Pre-Employment Tests Can Help #HR Hire Faster (and Better). HR Bartender, Sharlyn Lauby, February 2017

most people don't want to be approached in private or personal space. You will also lack good outbound recruiting data because you won't get consistent inputs; some people don't indicate where they work, and you may get data that isn't relevant or you shouldn't be collecting, for example, ethnic background or religion.

When it comes to other social media tools and their application for Talent Acquisition, be aware of the risks, and value each bring. Instagram for example can be used very effectively to communicate about your employer brand. It has not proven itself as a place to find corporate talent.

Pinterest can also carry some weight as an employer branding tool. You can pin many things to the board including employee pictures, employee-created articles, video, PowerPoint presentations, and these can be easily found through Google. Like the previously mentioned tools, it does not hold a lot of power to source talent though and does not generate dialogue.

Google Plus can help you to prioritize search and may help your brand be easier to find. It makes sense to have and maintain a destination for careers to help people find you easily – and it's free (more to come on free tools in Chapter 6).

Snapchat has been used as an outreach tool for branding or targeting a market, or vertical to attract through video. A global fast food chain has seen success in attracting restaurant workers through this medium. They buy data confirming age, location, and tag specific interests as the tool is very targeted for audience segments. You can also use paid ads to run video and target specific groups.

Personally, I have found the aforementioned social media tools less accurate than ads run in LinkedIn, which remains one of the top social tools for recruiting. There are a few additional sections in this book dedicated to using LinkedIn effectively, so more to come on that.

Recently, my company, Riviera Advisors has invested in a mix of Instagram, Facebook, and Twitter. We use them to promote content and blogs, reach our desired audiences, and listen to the industry conversation around us. All in all, if you're going to use social media, be sure to make your strategy specific to the cohort you want to reach, and keep track of who is following/linking/sharing your content as a litmus test to see if you are getting your desired results and if your social media investments are making your team more efficient. If you are going to be investing in a social media strategy, a social media management tool such as Hootsuite is very important to include in your Talent Acquisition social media strategy since it will help automate and manage the many channels you will need to administer.

EVALUATING YOUR NEEDS FOR TOOLS AND TECHNOLOGY

Tools and technology are a must for your success today. I have not come across a team that has been successful without at least a few tools to help them focus on their core work. It's all about relationships and with the right mix, and balance of tools, your time can be spent with people – be it your internal clients and partners, or the candidates themselves. Recruiters need a balance as well, and they need to see how the tools can empower them to do their job more effectively without fear of being replaced. Here are a few high-level considerations while you evaluate your tool mix.

- Have you identified which processes are taking up the most of your team's time and if a tool could solve the issue?

- If you were a candidate your company desired, would their experience be improved by the use of technology?

- Does your team understand the vision of using the tools and their full capabilities?

- How long would it take to transition to a tool and what is your change management plan?

- Will your use of tools hinder your team, or candidates in any way?

- Can you optimize your tools to help you weed out candidates who are not suitable – since many open the doors to let anyone apply for any role they choose?

By reducing the amount of manual work that Recruiters have on a day-to-day basis, it allows them to focus on higher-value tasks. With this mix in mind, I encourage you to visit RecruitCONSULT.net for an up to date listing of available tools, and some commentary on my experience implementing these tools with my clients. Keep in mind the list is not exhaustive, and that I focus on tools meant for medium and large organizations. There may be some great tools out there for small businesses, or ones with a leaner HR organization, for example startups.

During the needs assessment process my clients often ask for a benchmark on spending, or for a list of tools competitors use. It's important to focus your evaluation of tools on their usefulness above all else. Always keep the focus on how a tool can optimize or improve, that can take away a heavy lift, or drastically reduce your time spend so that you can improve the underlying time, cost, or quality of the Talent Acquisition services you provide. This means a level of diligence must be exercised so you find the right balance for your business. I have seen companies go wild and purchase every tool available on the market. Their Recruiters end up spending too much time on training and bouncing back and forth between tools. Make sure your suite of tools can integrate as much as possible so you're not wasting time. We can easily get caught up in all the bells and whistles and shiny objects offered and the thoughtfulness around how the tools are implemented into daily life are not considered. If I'm a Recruiter, and I have to go into tools that each stand as a separate contained entity all day, I won't get any work done. You must focus on finding the tools and technology that give you a significant lift on *improving speed, cost, quality and pipeline.* These four things help create the ideal Rubik's Cube for Talent Acquisition tools.

Investing time in your tool mix is important because do-overs are rare. If you implement tools and technology that do not improve speed, cost, quality, and pipeline, people will not use the tools because they will be too cumbersome. If your ATS works with video interviewing, chatbots, onboarding tools, and background screening processing, you're giving time back to your teams and more strategic manpower to the business. The more you can bolt on tools and features, the better. Without this, it is a recipe for failure. Recruiters' number one job is to recruit. If we don't have time for them to do this job because they are bogged down with tools, training to learn to use the tools, or a steep learning curve that makes them weary which tools, we won't be successful at our job. All to say, be very careful which tools and technology you select, and use your standard metrics to know for certain if the mix you select provides your team the lift you set out to achieve.

READINESS AND TRAINING

Have you ever come across a tool that you thought would transform all you did, and then had it fail miserably? I've seen clients become so committed to the tool that they have lost sight of its transformative possibilities for the team. I want to encourage you to invest in a strategic change management plan with a focus on communication. You'll later get to a chapter dedicated to change management, so this next part is specifically directed to change management with regards to tools and technology. If you want your tools and technology to improve speed, cost, quality and pipeline, you have to ensure that both the tools, and those using the tools are properly prepared. I worked with a client who had a need to invest in their university recruiting efforts. They found a resource that automated this type of recruiting that promised to remove the need to have an on-campus presence, so they invested a large sum of money. Behind this resource, there was very little interaction with candidates, and the Recruiters were not prepared to invest more time as the tool was supposed to free up portions of their day. The company was not ready to hone the relationships that were initiated by this tool and were not able to connect with people. The tool of course, could not connect with people and without integration to other tools the team was using, this university recruiting tool turned out to be an expensive, clunky mess that was not easy to use, and cost more time, money, did not enhance quality and did not enhance pipeline in a positive way. My client retired the use of the tool (which was also very low because of a lack of immediate results) and the experience was a deemed a lesson learned.

Part of the allure of using many tools is that at times, large enterprise solution software companies offered additional services for 'free'. After they created their ATS, service providers would include other underlying systems (HRIS, Payroll, etc.). While they might specialize in an ATS, the additional services would often be sub-par, especially in terms of user experience. I encountered a system such as this that a client of mine was trying to implement. In having a Recruiter show me their daily experience, I was stunned to see that the system required the Recruiter to lift their hand 50-100 times each time they needed to complete a process – per candidate! There were a lot of drop down menus, a lot of fields that did not auto populate, and a lot of clicking was required to get to the next screen. The user experience was terrible and the Recruiter shared with me that they, and their peers tended not to want to use it, so they cut corners, put minimal info, and turned the system into a paperweight. Since the users were not using the systems in their intended ways, it added less and less value, and sucked up more and more time.

The big "aha" moment for this Talent Acquisition leader was that while Recruiters are notorious lovers of technology initially – they quickly turn to shiny bright objects. They love webinars on the latest tools coming out – when it comes to use, they are actually notoriously against technology. It simply takes too much work. To find a happy medium for those who love and soon hate technology, understand that your Recruiters may or may not love to use new tools, and that overall, they don't love to spend a lot of time on inputting data.

Another client I worked with charged full speed ahead and purchased product licenses for a product that promised to 'do it all' through the recruiting process. They thought that they could tell Recruiters it was available, and flip a switch to turn the tool on and it would immediately optimize their operation. After all, this is how the product was sold to them and there were numerous case studies of success – they were very excited to reap the benefits. Unfortunately, they didn't anticipate the level of change required by the back office team that was to use this great new tool, and training was minimal. It took longer than expected to get the team operational, employees did not feel like they were part of the journey, and it caused pain and angst between leadership resulting in an additional, and tangible slowdown in the work that was supposed to be sped up. The important lesson is to always invest the time in planning for change, bringing people along on your journey, and not assuming that others will be as supportive of the change, either initially, or later in the game.

ACCOUNTABILITY FOR TALENT ACQUISITION TECHNOLOGY AND TOOLS

Remember tools and technology are an important part of enabling you to get your strategy implemented. They do not replace the need for you to interact with your team, ask questions, probe, and keep a focus on personal relationships. Your system for collecting the data you need to be a strategic advisor should be as optimized as your team is. The right mix of internal and external tools and technology will enable you to be as efficient as possible. And remember, you will likely have an IT partner who is there to help you as well. Get them on board early for best results.

Once the right tools and technology are in place, they will require upkeep as well. They are evolving ecosystems that your team will need to guide to the right spaces. Don't let yourself become the point of contact for all technology and tool challenges – there could be many, even with the best of systems and integrations. Having to tell your stakeholders they are not seeing you, or not feeling supported because you and your team are so wrapped up in tools is never a good place to be. Ensure you have the right resources and support in place, and that your organization is ready to optimize the use of the tools. You are accountable for the work that is output through your team, and the way the work gets done to ensure success is part of this. While the technology team will be your partner, it will be the Talent Acquisition leader who will own the tools, the vendor relationships, and the reponsibility to prove that it works.

CONCLUSION

There are a lot of tools out there—some will help you optimize your function, others may simply create noise in your system. It's your job as the RecruitCONSULT! leader to ensure that all of your resources are best used, best supported, and best implemented. Try taking an inventory of your tools and technology every year to ensure you are using what you have, and getting the data that you need from your suite of tools. Talk to the users first – they will give you the insights you need to make the right decisions and then bring your team along on your journey to improving speed, cost, quality and pipeline.

CHAPTER 3: TALENT ACQUISITION ANALYTICS, MAKING SENSE OF ALL THE DATA

With the right set of tools and technology in place, you have a lot of data available to you. Information is great – not knowing what to do with it, or how to collect it, is not so great. I'll give you a few examples of areas that will be helpful in setting up the tools and technology you've invested in, and making sure you are able to tease out the metrics your partners will need in order to know you're in a position to find the best talent today, and tomorrow. Applying analytics correctly will greatly influence your ability to tell the story of the talent landscape for your organization and keep you in the position of expert.

Let me share with you an example of why analytics are so important. The story starts with an Applicant Tracking System (ATS). This tool has a ton of data in it, and gets thousands of elements that are both submitted and stored within. You can get lots of data on requisitions, sources of where your candidates are coming from, and information about the people you've interviewed. There is so much data it can be hosted on its own server. With so much information, you need to know how to use it to help predict success or make investments – and truly, how to inform the business strategy.

PREDICTING INSTEAD OF GUESSING

Predictive analytics are the outcome of using data to make informed projections of what could happen in the future. Big data analytics have been instrumental in changes to workforce forecasting, identifying the source of attrition, targeting available talent, and defining profiles of successful candidates.

With the availability of such useful information, industries have not only been able to improve their own internal practices and performance, but also better benchmark across industries. It can mean we all get better, or simply that the divide between what is 'good' and what is 'bad' is much more obvious. It's another way to get scientific and empirical about our own performance and the value Talent Acquisition is bringing to the business.

While there will always be new buzz words in the industry, the practice of using data to better prepare for the future is not a new concept. Early examples would be using the infamous ink blot test developed by Hermann Rorschach, to see what candidates saw with each abstract picture and use that data to predict what the response might mean in terms of job performance.

If you can take the guesswork out, this is another way to save time and come to the table with evidence-based data to influence the business positively. It's important that you know what the data means and how to interpret it properly. Doing this can reveal issues with your talent pipeline you didn't see coming, just as easily as it can show you that your team is over-functioning in some areas.

PULLING VALUABLE INSIGHTS FROM VAST AMOUNTS OF INFORMATION

I once worked with a client whose workforce was made up of a large portion of hourly line workers. They hired many people who did service work in call centers for account questions and support. This team was looking for ways to optimize their hiring of this type of talent, by seeing how well they did through the year-long training that was required to be successful in the role. They started to look at past experience, but this area was not a deep source of information as many of the candidates had short experience profiles and frankly, this was not a role that required deep experience. We set out to use their analytics to predict how well people will respond to the year-long training required as one specific data point. We looked at their classroom experience, on the job performance, certifications, and licenses first, then measured that against successful employees. In this instance, with such a wide potential candidate pool, they had to figure out what past experience might predict future success to help pull valuable insights as to how long people would need to get up and running, predicting turnover and when that might happen, and use that to ensure staffing levels were always suitable.

What they learned was that a certain percentage of staff would turn over at the 6-8 month timeframe, then again between 9-11 months. If they the employee was still there at the 14 month mark, a large percent of those employees would stay long term. With this information, they were better able to predict a hiring model and confidently assess how many people they need to recruit. Using custom made assessment tools for job previews, the team came to understand success practices of new employees in their life cycle at the company and using data from their first 18 months, accurately predict success.

Be aware that when you have a larger number of employees, it will be easier to use analytics to help with success. This is because the patterns can become more obvious, faster than when you have a smaller number. In other roles, it can be much more difficult. The important part is to leverage the insights you do have that can scale, and find the immediate opportunities, or so called 'lower hanging fruit' to leverage value where you can.

Whether your organization uses analytics for a better understanding of your hiring process, retention, success factors of employees, turnover, or succession planning, there is a strong use case for all.

ANALYTICS FOR A COMPETITVE EDGE

Great leaders are prepared, and they work really hard to minimize chaos for their teams. They make thoughtful plans with the input of many, and they have backup plans should things go wrong. They also approach data as a tool to be able to tell stories about humans, and don't take a data-driven approach to treat people like figures.

Common practices across the industry identify the main uses for talent analytics as: human capital facts, analytical HR, human capital investment analysis, workforce forecasts, the talent value model and the talent supply chain. Human capital facts are the original data points involving individuals in the organization. An investment in this area analyzes the actions taken from analytical HR in order to see which had or have the greatest impact on the organization. You can earn a competitive edge using this data to look at hiring, retention, turnover, and succession in order to strategically plan for any potential gaps or surpluses in the workforce *before they happen*. The talent supply chain, while the most complex part of using HR analytics, is by far the best solution. It allows organizations to understand the data, the analysis, and make talent related decisions based off of what they know. Each of these six pieces of the HR analytics puzzle is beneficial to the organization as a whole, but using all six together, and correctly, would provide a huge positive impact to the company.

Mastering the topic of talent analytics takes a great deal of understanding the fundamentals or DELTA [5]: data, enterprise, leadership, targets, and ana-

5   *The Big Idea: Competing on Talent Analytics,* Thomas H. Davenport, Jeanne Harris, and Jeremy Shapiro, October 2010
https://www.harvardbusiness.org/sites/default/files/HBR_Competing_on_Talent_Analytics.pdf

lysts. Each piece of DELTA is an important piece to understand. When they work together, they enable your team to operate from a more analytical point of view.

I have a client that is a very high-tech company and they enter into new markets regularly. As a publicly traded company, they report on Wall Street when they have new products in the pipeline to let investors know that in two years, something big will be available. This is a normal business occurrence; however, the business neglected the important step of bringing Talent Acquisition into their careful planning and execution of this announcement. The business as a whole did not have a good grasp of DELTA. When the discussion of what kind of local talent would be needed to build and execute this new product, they neglected to look into data on the skills they would need. As there had been no sourcing done and the talent was not readily available in the marketplace, they were facing a major challenge. They didn't even have enough global information about the type of talent in order to execute on the business need that had now been announced publicly.

From inside the company, the head of Talent Acquisition got an excited call from the business lead to share that they were ready to launch the product. This person told me all about the regulatory approvals obtained in Europe, and how the business lead told them to proceed 'full steam ahead' to fill the roles they would need. Talent Acquisition was not ready though and had to reply with an apology and the news that they were not in a position to get the desired talent right away. It was a big 'oops' moment on many sides – the company now needed critical people that they promised Wall Street would be hired so the plan could be executed, but nobody talked to Talent Acquisition. Even if they had two years prior, the people then in Talent Acquisition wouldn't have been able to share the type of people available because they didn't share an Applicant Tracking System. The basic fundamentals of analytics were not in place to be tracked, and without any longevity, there were no patterns or discernable data points to help them find key talent. As a result, Talent Acquisition was forced to blindly estimate how many people with the desired skills and experience were available in their local areas. They would've had this info at their fingertips had they been able to mine jobs from the past. They didn't invest in inputting certain critical data in their system for the future and it had a drastic impact on the business.

In another industry not too far away, my clients had a different experience when they used their data analytics predictively to earn a competitive edge. They knew that in five years, their Talent Acquisition team would have to do certain things to keep the organization at the forefront of their industry. They would need to source and hire people in key roles that were most important to the business. Roles like R&D Scientists and Regulatory Managers would be in high demand and without them, the business would not thrive. My client knew they would have to do all the searches in a global Talent Acquisition system – so they would have a global view on how many candidates per job, time to fill, and which strategy would help them predict and manage future strategies. Overall, they knew there were many things to be done with analytics.

With this knowledge and a strategic plan to use the information they had available at that moment, they were ready. Not surprisingly, this team was successful, not only domestically, but globally. They set up talent communities, built relationships with university programs, and identified the skills required so they didn't have to take such a narrow view of talent they would be looking for. The Talent Acquisition team hired on time, at a lower cost, and transcended geographic boundaries to get the best talent for the team. Starting early as a partner with the right tools to help the business succeed was how they were able to achieve greatness. And the team was happy to take those gold stars the business was throwing at them.

HIRING BY ALGORITHMS

If you are the Talent Acquisition lead today, you can spend a good portion of time in a database. You can come out with a lot of ideas to create operational opportunities for your team. You should be investing this time in this activity, and you should be doing it with a plan. You can use this to change resources, improve mentoring/coaching, and to build development plans for your team. It can also show you where you might need to supplement your organization with outside resources, or help you decide which outsourcing will be most effective for your team. Analytics are a facet of operational excellence that you need to know in order to improve and optimize your team.

The Recruiters on your team should do the same and will be more effective than their peers with your direction. They will convert a higher number of sourced candidates versus working from an empty slate. They will be better able to engage with their Hiring Managers, and have a higher acceptance rate of candidates.

The data, and the understanding of that data gathered over time can help to determine your talent pipeline and availability of talent within that pipeline. It can help you describe which sources are delivering the best talent to your organization. It can even influence your strategy to hire by algorithm[6], which has been proven effective in many areas. One specific example was the manager of a baseball team who had a superstar roster with high paid, high profile players, but a long losing streak despite these things. After that season, the General

6   *Big Data, Predictive Analytics and Hiring,* Glenn Rifkin, May 12, 2014
https://www.kornferry.com/institute/big-data-predictive-analytics-and-hiring

Manager decided to make a drastic change to help snap the losing streak. He traded several superstar players for players with specific talents, even if they were not fantastic overall like the superstars. The General Manager focused on good chemistry and team fit instead of well-known all around talent – all information found in the baseball equivalent of an ATS. The strategy paid off and the team went from the bottom of the league to World Series Champions within a season. In addition, tracking data and using data analysis, people from within the HR department can look at recruiting metrics such as time to fill and cost of vacancy in order to see how their productivity is affecting the bottom line for the organization. Hiring by algorithms ultimately enables you to build a team that can work well together based on predictive data points, even if they aren't all considered the very best in their field.

USING DATA TO TELL YOUR TALENT ACQUISITION STORY

The previous example provided a really specific way of finding specialized talent to build a superior baseball team. There are several other ways to use your data strategically so you don't get lost in the vast sea of talent information. A RecruitCONSULT! leader will always have an eye out for ways to optimize their Talent Acquisition operation. As we all know, our teams will often have limited resources and we want to make the most of them. Truly, we *have* to make the most of them. Earlier in the book, we talk about prioritization of jobs. This info can help build awareness for the skill set and understanding of the most difficult to source. Maybe the data tells you you're not very good at converting these sourced candidates into hires. Maybe you need outsourcing, or insourcing, but look at how many sourced candidates it takes to get a hire. For example, if you have a sourcing resource and they present prospects to Recruiters, and Recruiters pass them on to the Hiring Managers and they don't turn into hires, it's wasting a lot of time and money. Conversion rates on sourced candidates, and sources of candidate come through all channels. If I'm spending $100,000 every quarter on all channels and talent attraction tools, and all of them are bringing in candidates, data will certainly tell me which is the most successful. One of them has to be the leader in the number of conversions. When we boil it all down, half of the hires come from one place (i.e., referrals, or job boards). That suggests that you might want to more heavily invest in the places that work best, and stop investing where you receive less return on investment. You have to look at it over a period of time. If you invest $10,000 each month on a job site, some months, you may not have jobs on that site. In that month, you're not getting a fantastic return on investment, but that doesn't mean that the channel is bad. It means you may not have candidates in the pipeline, or haven't needed to hire for six months. The data tells that story today and can as well tomorrow. Source effectiveness is one area that can really influence an overall Talent Acquisition team's effectiveness.

Another way to let your data help influence your strategy is to look at some of your roles at the core of your business. Let's say you need to hire a lot of sales and commercial jobs. You can use your ATS tool to mine data, but you can also look at data from your current sales employees. You will likely have information available to you as to where the top performers came from, who have lasted the longest, who have performed the best over time, and where were they sourced from. You can look at where they came from, what type of companies, and what kinds of experiences they gained before they came to your organization. You can also look at what training and learning they've been through, and how all this data can predict their success in your environment. You can even go into their formal education and see what schools have produced the talent you need and which programs they studied. As we've seen this transformation over time, it's not only business school graduates that can be wildly successful in the right culture. Now you can work your strategy from the viewpoint of all these great nuggets of information that are available to you.

A word of caution, especially if your company is a federal contractor and therefore is subject to Office of Federal Contract Compliance Programs (OFCCP) compliance regulations. These great nuggets of data are anecdotal from a strictly legal perspective unless and until your company commits additional resources to go through a formal process to prove the data point(s) are predictive of good employee performance and therefore acceptable to be used as stand-alone candidate selection criteria. Unless you've gone through the effort and expense of proving certain data points are predictive, use of these data points as the sole selection criteria could be very problematic. Instead, I recommend using these data points as additional factors to be considered in the selection process, but not the only criteria.

DATA ABOUT YOUR CURRENT TALENT

I mentioned insourcing, and when looking inside the company, referral programs come to mind (and I'll mention that outsourced services can manage these for you as well). In referral programs, in addition to creating a place your existing employees want to work, so that they will tell others how much they enjoy working there – you also want them to refer people they will be proud to work beside. As you start to collect referrals, the data they provide can also help influence your strategy and you can work that into your successful program design.

I had a client who developed products and was very big on innovation as part of their culture. They wanted people who were excited about building, trying, and learning along with them. They invested their time in data mining to understand why in some jobs, their referral program was much more successful than other sources. They decided to more heavily invest in this area and considered it low hanging fruit as the data told them their teams were engaged, and were driven by previous incentives.

They targeted key talent roles, and for each employee referral, there was an entry into a draw for a company-paid two year lease on a BMW vehicle. And they did this each quarter! By targeting a specific population, they significantly increased not just referrals, but their success rate in converting these referrals as the right fit for talent in their organization. They used the same sales analytics, conversion projections, and commercial analytics as a marketing function, but applied it to recruiting. It was almost the same concept and yielded very similar results. If you're a great marketer or brand manager, you will look at the sales analytics and which social media gets the best engagement, and which coupon gets the most conversion from which markets. For Talent Acquisition, we can apply the same strategy for fantastic results too.

CONCLUSION

I liken analytic tools to our version of a crystal ball that yields empirical data. None of us know what the future will bring, which is why it is crucially important to be prepared for the areas we can predict. Analytics can be daunting if you don't take the right approach and useless if you aren't able to pull out the valuable insights that are available to you and your team. You can implement all the tools in the world, but if they don't help you improve your ability to understand, find insights, or help you find gaps, they are worthless. The RecruitCONSULT! approach is to bring value to the business, and being able to show, in quick and easy ways, how that value comes to life in the success of the business. Remember that while analytics are often helping you predict and influence for future actions, there will always be some element of reaction when you deal with people. The more you can get out of your analytics to help influence how you will find the talent your organization needs today and tomorrow, the more you can build the right programs that ensure your team is working on the highest value tasks.

CHAPTER 4: METRICS AND ECONOMICS

Earlier, I talked about the importance of being able to measure, and also being sure you are giving your client exactly what they want and not every number you can produce.

Measurement of Talent Acquisition is the end result of analytics – analyze the data available to you.

In the Talent Acquisition world, we love to discuss the *idea* of measuring our performance. But even though most Talent Acquisition leaders know they *should* measure their Talent Acquisition success, they don't *do* it.

There are many reasons for this, the most important being that we are often so busy with what is directly in front of us, that we don't make the time to develop our metrics and measurements. Or it just seems too complex. In some cases, leaders just don't want to measure their success because frankly they are afraid of what the numbers may reveal.

The first step in the metrics game is to go to the business managers and ask, "How will you measure the success of our Talent Acquisition processes?" Don't just ask the top managers: ask the department managers, supervisors, and unit leaders (i.e., your Hiring Managers).

Nine times out of ten, they will tell you the two key metrics that matter most are *speed and quality*. Not interview-to-hire ratios, not quality of source, and surprisingly, not even cost.

When HR and Talent Acquisition leaders answer these same questions, they almost always start with cost. But in reality, when you're looking at what's most important overall in increasing the value of the business, recruiting costs are typically not as important as *speed* and *quality* of Talent Acquisition's processes.

An important issue to remember is that if the costs of gathering and presenting the metrics outweigh any possible results that would stem from them, don't waste your time and money. Recognize that someone else's idea of a best practice is *not* a best practice if it doesn't fit within your own organization.

But in the long run, remember that the fundamental potency of metrics lies in the following statement:

You cannot improve what you don't measure.

So, stop the procrastinating and let's get down to the process of measuring. Before you start, recognize that the most important thing is developing practices that fit within *your* organization. So rather than getting all bent out of shape trying to figure out various complicated metrics in a vacuum that may cost you lots of time and money, take the first, most important step: ask your business what is important to them. How will they measure the success of their Recruiting and Talent Acquisition processes? You will then have real-time trend data you can use to craft some simple, top-level metrics from which the whole business—not just those in HR and recruiting—will benefit.

A Lesson from the Real World

When I was first starting out in HR I worked in a hotel. I was in a job where I was responsible for managing employee benefits and employee safety. I didn't really enjoy the job, but I was good at it.

On the employee safety side, we had to report employee "lost time" injuries on an update we sent to the corporate office. Every month our hotel (one of more than eighty around the world) was ranked on a list that was distributed by the corporate office. If we had more injuries, we ranked lower, and if we had fewer injuries, we ranked higher.

I was constantly under pressure to put programs and systems in place to move our ranking higher up on that report since our General Manager really cared about the results and his bonus depended on it. If I put programs and systems in place that worked we saw the results—fewer injuries and happy employees (and a happy General Manager, which meant a happy me!)

Then the hotel's Director of HR promoted me to running Talent Acquisition (Staffing at that time). In this job I was responsible for Talent Acquisition ensuring our hotel had the right number of employees. I really enjoyed this position, and it gave me a taste of my future passion.

But this job did not have any corporate reporting requirements. In fact, there were no reports to run at all. There were no real measures of success; only that my "customers" (the hotel's managers) were happy with the work I was doing. I was really excited about my new passion of providing Talent Acquisition, but had no real way to prove my success to the corporate office and the people outside our little 500 employee hotel.

So, as a young upstart, I spent hours of my own time on the computer trying to come up with some measurements and metrics that I could use to garner attention. I was successful: I came up with all sorts of measurements such as "interviews to hire," "cost per hire," "cost for recruiting by department," "vacancy rate." I spent hours and hours creating reports.

My boss and our General Manager were thrilled by these reports, and so was I, because I could see my results and show success from one period to another. I did so well with this that it got the attention of the corporate office. And, fairly soon thereafter, I got a promotion to run part of recruiting at the corporate level. There I got to actually implement some of my metrics at the more than eighty other properties around the world. As we say in HR, I got to "roll them out" to the field. Now all of the other 80 Talent Acquisition managers would have to spend hours and hours of their time filling out reports and forms and tracking all this information so we could roll it all up to the corporate office. Every month I could have a huge fancy report that I would distribute to all of our executives. It was really impressive—to me. Just like a CPA who toils for extra hours every month at month-end closing, I (along with our entire organization of Talent Acquisition people) would spend hours preparing the documentation for these metrics reports. My HR bosses loved the reports and the data.

One day I spent some time out in the field with one of our Senior Vice Presidents of Operations. I really wanted to let him know that I was the guy who developed all of those great Talent Acquisition reports that he received every month. I asked him what he thought of the reports and the data. His response was a turning point for me. He said, "I don't read those ridiculous reports, Jeremy! I don't have time for that. Here's the deal: all I care about is getting the best employees we can, as soon as I can get them. Period. All of those reports and work you spend—frankly, I don't care. I want results."

A light bulb went off in my head. Measure only what's important to the business and what you intend to use to help you improve your results. Period.

What I have learned over my more than 25 years in this profession is that much of the time and resources we spend on measuring our work goes to our friends and colleagues in HR. The corporate executives rarely see the data, don't have time to read it, and don't really care.

The trick is to ask the business leaders how they measure Talent Acquisition success, and then the rest will follow.

PRACTICAL METRICS

In Talent Acquisition, measuring nothing is obviously not an option. Measuring everything, as I tried to do in my hotel career, is not the answer either.

You need to be able to evaluate progress, and for that you need metrics that are meaningful, easy to understand, and directly relate to the bottom line.

Of useful measurements there are two broad categories:

1. Organizational metrics

These are metrics that report what your business leaders tell you is important to them. They are related to the quality of the candidates and new hires and the time it takes to get someone hired, as well as constituent satisfaction (Hiring Managers, new hires, and candidates not hired). They may therefore be somewhat subjective.

In addition, these measurements may also include such things as overall costs or a percentage of costs compared to annualized salaries hired. These metrics are ones that help organizations "sell" and prove the value of their internal Talent Acquisition functions.

New-hire quality is one of the most difficult metrics for Talent Acquisition leaders and HR professionals to get their heads around. My view is simply this: new-hire quality is measured by how well the new employees are performing relative to how the organization expects their performance to be. Every job must have specific, measurable accountabilities that must be achieved within a certain measurable period of time. Generally, I believe that this time frame is within six months of a new employee's hire. Each new recruiting assignment must begin with the Recruiter working with the Hiring Manager to identify four to six key accountabilities for the new employee to achieve within that first six-month period. After the six-month period is over, the Recruiter or the Talent Acquisition team can go back to each manager who had a new hire in that period and ask (either directly or via a survey) how well the new employee performed.

This process does two things: it forces the Recruiter to draw out effective accountabilities for each job from the Hiring Manager and it allows the Recruiter to know what accountabilities will be required so that they can create effective sourcing, screening, and assessment mechanisms to identify those accountabilities from a candidate's past performance.

Constituent satisfaction metrics look at satisfaction from the constituencies of the Talent Acquisition function: Hiring Managers, candidates (people who were interviewed but not hired—this could be for rejected candidates or candidates who turn down the organization's offer), and new hires (people who were hired recently). These metrics are typically designed to gather specific feedback through anonymous survey tools that can then be used to track trends and opportunities for change in an unbiased way. There are even companies that will allow organizations to participate in standard surveys that

JEREMY M. ESKENAZI | 45

can be compiled with similar industry data for benchmarking purposes.

Collecting data from both candidates who were selected and those who were not selected provides a perspective that internal Talent Acquisition people rarely get. The information reveals what they are thinking about the process and the employer brand. Many Recruiters are terrified of this metric, but fortunately, the first time is the most difficult. Baseline it first and build your matrix of expectations.

The organizational metrics—which are fewer in number than the efficiency metrics—yield results that the CEO and other executive leaders of the hotel chain would be interested in knowing. But keep reports brief. A good rule of thumb is that if the CEO cannot read and understand your report in thirty seconds, it is too long.

2. Efficiency metrics

These are the types of measurements Talent Acquisition and HR leaders may use to manage internal processes, problems, and issues with methods and systems. These tend to be more objective and numbers-driven metrics and typically include measuring things such as individual Recruiter productivity, vacancy/fill rates, sourcing effectiveness, internal cycle times (i.e., how long it takes to present candidates to a Hiring Manager), and certain cost elements.

This information is only important to you as a leader if you can do something with the data. It will help you to identify issues that need correcting and improving as well as helping to manage your internal performance. These measurements can also be very time-consuming to collect and difficult to analyze. They can be the type of metrics that can make a Talent Acquisition leader's head spin while they are getting those requisitions filled and trying to "keep the train moving."

These metrics are often easy to acquire through a sophisticated talent/ Application Tracking System (ATS) but require 100% Recruiter compliance to enter status data.

> **Operational metrics** include cycle time (time to hire, time to target), efficiency (interview funnel, offer/accept ratio), and source effectiveness (how effective the sources of your applicants are compared to others).

> **Cost metrics** include cost per hire (CPH), recruiting efficiency ratio (the ratio between the overall costs to acquire candidates and the total annualized salaries for those hired), and cost per source.

Beware of the Cost-Per-Hire Metric
A lot of HR and Talent Acquisition leaders love to quote the ubiquitous

CPH metric. The metric is seemingly simple: divide the number of jobs filled by the overall cost to fill all the jobs. Everyone has heard the old saying, "Numbers don't lie." Perhaps not, but they can be misleading when not considered in the proper context. If you are comparing data across an organization with more than one location, or in more than one industry, you need to make sure that you are aware of potential variances such as:

Geographic differences—variances in the cost of living and costs of services in different geographies make the per-hire comparisons difficult.

Industry differences— some industries have more difficulty attracting candidates than others.

Functional differences—per-hire measures fail to account for variation of type of positions. CPH is not meaningful to organizations that hire into many different types of positions.

Differences in job levels—compensation varies by level; per-hire measures are not conducive to comparisons between positions at different levels.

The CPH metric is so difficult because until recently, there has been no set standard on what the metric really means (what costs should be included in the overall costs, for example). The Society for Human Resources Management (SHRM) developed an internationally accepted standard for this metric to hopefully put some standardization to this process. You can read more about this standard at RecruitCONSULT!.net. However, I don't like CPH as a metric because in the end it doesn't really tell me a lot about my work. It can help me plan and develop my budgets more effectively, but again, it should be an internal operational metric, not one that is reported on to the business.

The interview-to-hire/funnel model tells you how many interviews it takes to get hires. It also provides the interview-to-hire ratio and the applicant-to-hire ratio. This is helpful in planning for resources, time, and other factors, and it can also be used to see how well Recruiters are assessing candidates that they prescreen before they are presented to the Hiring Managers.

The efficiency metrics listed above yield data that the CEO of the company and other executive leaders of the company are not going to be interested in or have time to read. They are strictly for the Talent Acquisition function's in-house consumption.

FUNDING THE TALENT ACQUISITION FUNCTION

It's a fact of life that while the most important thing is to create a high-quality, effective Talent Acquisition function, one can't ignore the cost and how it's funded. The way a Talent Acquisition organization is funded can create a certain dynamic between Talent Acquisition professionals and clients, which can make for a healthier recruiting environment and help you do your job better. The dynamic could be more exchange-based using a pay-per-hire model, or more socialist in nature where the services are provided to all who need with no additional exchange of budgets internally. You could actually get your Talent Acquisition organization funded by someone else and, in doing so, be more effective. It's all about your value to the company.

Small Companies

Small companies usually fund Talent Acquisition in a very straightforward way. There isn't much money so everybody's neck is on the line. Thus, they usually go the simple and traditional route: all recruiting costs, including outside third-party searches, fall under HR. This includes the permanent, fixed costs of Recruiter salaries, job postings, advertising, recruitment advertising, job fairs, and costs associated with technology, such as ATS. Typically, this also includes the cost of outside third-party Recruiters (if it isn't put into an outside line item called "unbudgeted cost" that gets absorbed by HR). Occasionally small companies will have third-party Recruiters paid by the business areas who hired them. But generally, with small companies all costs are owned by HR.

Big Companies

In big companies, Talent Acquisition activities are not always funded by HR—it's not even smart for HR to own all the recruiting costs. In this instance money does not translate into power. However, as in every instance, value does.

Here's the problem. In large companies, paradoxically, even though there's in theory more money and resources available to fund Talent Acquisition, the idea of large costs showing up on the "General and Administrative" (G&A) budget line is not attractive. If you have a big pot of money sitting on a line item like that in these environments, where do you think the company's going turn the minute they need to cut costs?

This is just one level – the crass, pure dollar amount level. But there's another downside to subsidizing your company's recruiting that's more fundamental and linked to your effectiveness as a valued partner. If you fund all the recruiting in your HR department, the service you provide your clients will, to them, essentially be "free." And we all know how we value something that's free versus something we have to pay for. So, to create a healthy Recruiter-client dynamic it's important that each side be vested in the process—that each has something to gain.

Thus, there are several reasons why it's important to know how to fund a corporate Talent Acquisition organization outside the traditional structure in a way that reflects a true cost-value relationship without having to expose external costs on the G&A line. "Okay, so how?" you ask. Well, as it turns out, there are several models to choose from that can be carved to fit your needs. Let's look at them, beginning with the ones that have been problematic. The upside is that many of these are becoming much more accepted because organizations are figuring out that chargeback models are good things to have.

1. Partial Chargeback

The first is a simple model that seems pretty straightforward and logical given the issues. If you're a head of Talent Acquisition and you're trying to create a Talent Acquisition function where you need to add Recruiters, technology, job posting, branding and an employee referral mechanism, you set it up where the overhead costs of Recruiters' salaries stay in HR but all other variable costs attributable to a search—such as advertising—get charged back to the business unit that's hiring.

Sounds logical, right? The problem is that sometimes it's difficult to assign certain costs to a department. For instance, when you have multiple searches for similar departments and you have to place a lot of ads you don't want to stick one department with the entire bill. Is this easily figured out? Of course, but it requires some judgment on what to do internally versus externally. And you still have that sizable chunk of overhead (Recruiters' salaries) on the dreaded G&A line.

2. Full Chargeback

In this scenario all Talent Acquisition costs are considered variable and are charged back to businesses. The costs are allocated to different business units based on the employee population or their percentage of the company's revenue. This also makes sense because a lot of other HR costs are allocated this way. It's simple, straightforward, but it's not very engaging. It doesn't really get either side vested in the process and outcome of Talent Acquisition. It becomes more difficult to develop those much needed relationships because it is a straight exchange. "I give you a list of needs; you deliver" is the mentality.

3. Allocation on a Per-Hire Basis

Not only does this method properly align recruiting with the businesses, it forces a planning conversation between Recruiters and the head of business units.

Here's what you do. In developing your budget for the quarter or year you sit down with your department heads to look at past and current turnover and determine future needs. Then you aggregate the numbers, come up with a demand forecast for the next quarter, and break it down by function and level. You now have the information to build out a recruiting strategy based on needs. You'll know your external, as well as internal, needs and how much funding you'll need per hire. Armed with an amount you can then go back to the Hiring Manager and present him/her with a figure. A key approach here is to present the amount you need to allocate to their department per hire, but then mention that whatever isn't used will be refunded or rebated. The great thing about this model overall is you could do it in advance, or on the back end after everything has occurred.

This may sound complicated but there are many benefits including:

- It forces dialogue between the Talent Acquisition professional and Hiring Manager before recruiting needs happen.

- It forces both sides to be equally invested in the process. There is mutual respect for the costs of recruiting, and it results in more engagement and investment in the process.

There are also several possible pitfalls:

- If the company is not used to having an allocation-chargeback model for other things; financial accounting could be an issue.

- Management and recruiting teams may not be able to do a good job forecasting needs (but they'll get better).

- It places the recruiting team in the difficult position of constantly having to sell their services internally (they'll need solid metrics related to time and quality).

- If you can't perform at a level the business units expect you to at cost-value, businesses will complain about those costs and go elsewhere, depriving you of the ability to maintain your department's overhead costs (the businesses won't have a chargeback).

- Some companies get into situations where they have to renegotiate their deal every quarter, which takes valuable time.

4. Retroactive Allocation

This model is a retroactive allocation of costs at the end of the year. The allocation is based not on a per-hire basis but as a percentage of the average salary of those you're recruiting.

For instance, if a department hires 100 people at an average salary of $85,000/year you could come up with a percentage to charge back—say 10%. So you would allocate $8,500/hire back to the business unit. And you could tier the percentage based on the level of the employees hired (the higher the level, the higher the percentage). In this model, because it's percentage-based, the HR department needs to be careful: they could end up making money.

5. Hybrid Fixed Cost Model

The last allocation model is a hybrid. At the beginning of the year you set it up to allocate your Talent Acquisition department's overhead fixed costs back to the businesses, and then as the year progresses, any specific costs above and beyond the overhead fixed are allocated to the businesses that used them.

CONCLUSION

"You cannot improve what you don't measure" is the foundation on which your metrics must be based. As a leader managing in the RecruitCONSULT! philosophy, you need to use the right metrics for two important reasons: to measure your own performance with the goal of constant improvement and to prove to your employer—the person who signs your paycheck—that you are providing exceptional value to the organization.

But wholesale metrics are not helpful to senior management. No executive has the time or patience to wade through a swamp of data. The metrics you choose to present must be concise and meaningful.

Does your Talent Acquisition function provide long-term value or is it just sucking up short-term costs? Are you using the right tools to ensure you can speak to this question? There are now an abundance of tools, plug-ins, dashboards, and apps you can use to help you get a clear picture, as I discussed in chapters two and three. The bottom line is that there are many ways to skin the allocation/chargeback cat. But the important thing is "skin in the game" for both the Talent Acquisition organization and the business unit. This is the path toward the Holy Grail for Talent Acquisition professionals: creating a high-quality Talent Acquisition function without outsourcing and on a zero-cost basis. Do that and you'll be a superhero! And then you're exactly where you want to be; you can focus on how to improve the performance of the Talent Acquisition function, not how to pay for it. You have analytics, you have strong metrics, and you're using technology! With all this great stuff in place, you may be thinking, now what? Let's get to the next chapter to continue on this journey.

CHAPTER 5: BUILDING THE CONSULTATIVE TALENT ACQUISITION TEAM

The jellyfish, having little means of propulsion, is at the mercy of the ocean's currents. Where the currents go, so does the jellyfish.

While for millions of years this arrangement has served jellyfish well, it is bad news for anyone in business—especially corporate Talent Acquisition professionals. In today's fast-paced and hyper-competitive economy, a passive approach is doomed to fail. The sharks will gobble you up.

In the Talent Acquisition industry order-takers are like jellyfish. They respond to conditions after the fact. When the boss suddenly announces, "Smithers has given his two weeks' notice! We need to hire a new Vice President of Marketing!" the order-taker sees this as something totally unexpected. Nevertheless, the order-taker dutifully responds by putting a job posting on the company website and looking on LinkedIn. Then the order-taker waits to see what resumes come in.

Two weeks later the boss knocks on the door. "Have we found anyone yet for that Vice President job? This is Smithers's last day. I need someone!"

The order-taker shrugs. "Sorry, boss. We've gotten a pile of resumes, but they're all from high school dropouts. No one is qualified." Sadly, the clueless order-taker has put the company's future in jeopardy.

The key is to lead a team of recruiting professionals who take a consultative approach in line with the RecruitCONSULT! philosophy. They cannot be mere order-takers. The team's task is to be clairvoyant and proactive. Clairvoyant because you need to be able to see into the future. You need to know that Smithers is unhappy even before he knows it. Proactive because you need to have a pool of candidates ready to contact the day Smithers announces he's leaving.

Unless your organization is small and you are a one-person Talent Acquisition shop, you will need a team. Your team needs to be as dedicated as you are to providing the best possible value to the organization.

Assembling your consultative Talent Acquisition team is not unlike putting together a sports team. You need to find the most highly skilled players who have the drive to win, and the willingness to set egos aside to reach the common goal… this is the RecruitCONSULT! philosophy.

TALENT ACQUISITION SKILL SETS

I'm a big believer that if you focus on a core set of skills necessary to do a job, any number of people with varying backgrounds can fill the role (of course you'll have to determine if they can fit into your culture). Recruiters in the past (and even still today) need great relationship, communication, sourcing, searching and technology skills. Recruiters today need to *add* skills in Project Management, social networking, teamwork, and political savvy capabilities, among others. Below is my quick and dirty list of some of the core skills necessary in hiring Recruiters:

- Communications skills (written and verbal)

- Relationship skills

- Project Management abilities

- Ability to be a strategic partner

- Self-starter/takes initiative

- Political savvy

- Computer/technology skills

- Social networking skills

- Searching, sourcing, other technical skills

- Creativity/innovative thinking

With this skill set in hand we can broaden the horizons of our profession and bring in new blood.

But before we search elsewhere let's take a moment to look in our own backyard and the issues one might face in recruiting from other Talent Acquisition environments. What are some of these environments?

• Third-party recruiting vendors (contingency, retained search firms)

• HR departments/internal Talent Acquisition teams

• Recruitment outsourcing firms (RPOs)

With respect to these professionals, the most critical issue you can address is; what can you do to lure a good Talent Acquisition professional away from their company to come work for yours. Here are two suggestions that I'll expand on in the next chapter, but will help ground your thinking as we continue:

1. Ensure that the job you're offering is one in which a Recruiter gets to *recruit*. Full life-cycle Recruiters handle everything from the intake with the Hiring Manager, to sourcing the candidates, to assessing the candidates to presenting and closing candidates. They really don't want to deal with "administrivia"—coordinating candidate travel and interviews, running reports, dealing with applicant tracking issues, and so on. (Don't get me wrong, all of those things are very important to the process.) But Recruiters want to recruit. The more that someone has logistical and administrative support (especially compared to their current role), the more attractive the opportunity to perhaps make a move.

2. Enable the Talent Acquisition professional to deal directly with the end client and be a strategic partner. Whether it's an in-house or third-party Recruiter, invariably they've had to go through at least one other party (such as an HR Generalist) before getting to the client. Enabling them to work closely with the ultimate client will be catnip to the high-quality Talent Acquisition professional.

Okay, this is all well and good, but we can only dip from the same well and recycle the same water for so long. To further the profession, we need to attract and develop the next generation of great Talent Acquisition professionals and bring in people with the skills we need. From where, you ask? Here are some other areas that may be attractive:

Project Management

A key skill set that we explore in greater detail in this chapter is project management. People with a project management focus would be individuals that could come from purchasing, logistics, or operations planning areas, among others. (I actually know a company that actively recruits project managers from construction and architecture firms to become Recruiters. It works immensely well, and this company has nothing to do with construction or architecture!) These professionals have great initiative, relationship management, and likely technical skills. They could also come from engineering or design firms or advertising agencies.

Sales and Marketing

Sales and marketing professionals have many of the skills I have mentioned. They're self-starters with strong relationship and Project Management skills. They're not as team-oriented, typically, but the trickier issue is you're sort of in a bind with sales people. If you recruit from within your own company, you don't want to "take out" the best sales people (also if they're true sales people and doing great they probably won't want to move) and yet you don't want a failed sales person. However, if anyone on your staff comes from sales it's often best to have sales people recruit other sales people.

Operations

Operations people may have many of the skills we seek, in particular Project Management and team/strategic-orientation skills. But the real advantage to having operations professionals as Recruiters is they typically recruit in their area of expertise. For instance, engineers recruit engineers, technology experts recruit technology experts. This expertise gives them a built-in credibility with Hiring Managers.

Management Trainee Programs

Many "academy" companies, such as consumer packaged goods, hospitality, retail, and rental car, have some sort of training program where they bring in newly minted college grads with promises of someday running the world—and getting paid handsomely for it. The problem (or opportunity for us) is that not everyone can be a manager and often after one or two years (the ideal time to approach someone from this area) a certain number of trainees will have realized they don't want to be in the industry they're in. Perhaps they could fit into our world?

Professional Service Pros (Legal, Accounting, Management Consulting)

It is very natural for someone from one of the service areas above to make the leap into Talent Acquisition. In fact, this is the area from which large search firms draw upon the most. People from these areas understand a service/strategic orientation, have solid communications skills, and are the ultimate project managers.

Stockbrokers/Real Estate Professionals

These individuals share many, if not most, of the characteristics of sales people. So, if they're a solid performer, compensation issues could be a factor. However, if they have struggled in a competitive market or the market suddenly cools, they could still have what it takes to be a great Recruiter. And bringing someone like that in-house, especially from the real estate business, would give them the stability they wouldn't otherwise have.

Writers

Writers are often great communicators, have strong sourcing and research skills, and are innovative self-starters. They also typically have competent interpersonal skills and are great project managers. Since the industry of Journalism has changed drastically, strong writers can often be found in Corporate Communication teams, freelancing, working as copy-writers, at a website, creative agency, or even as a freelance/staff writer or independent blogger. The common thread for writers is that often, you can attract them early in their career, and with this experience, you can lure them in knowing they can continue to use their skill set. In addition, compensation would likely be an improvement from their current state. I can tell you about several people I have personally hired in my past that I found from looking at the masthead of my local weekly business journal or favorite blog, and introducing myself to the paid-per-word author who hustles each week to get published. These people have been very excited to learn about an opportunity they never considered and have been successful. (You may need to start them out in the sourcing process and then later move them into full-cycle recruiting.)

Technical Education Teachers

Those from a community college or business/technical institutes (they even may be part-time or adjunct faculty) have many of the skills required.

What they may lack in business experience they make up for in substance. Communication, Project Management, and creativity/innovation skills are all strengths.

Political Campaign Workers

They are the ultimate project-managers, with savvy, great sourcing capabilities, and great relationship skills. A natural leap from the volatile (and not the most highly paid) world of politics.

College or University Admissions Professionals

They read a lot of backgrounds, they meet a lot of people, and they have lots of projects. They're not as savvy with corporate environments, so technical schools would be ideal.

The key to identifying and hiring outstanding team members is to think outside the box and look at the personality of the potential team member. Technical skills can be taught. It's important to hire people who can make your team grow and stretch – not just fit in today. We all know culture is malleable and a team of jellyfish will not help you lead a Talent Acquisition team to be the kind of organization it should be. You can teach any intelligent person how to build a database or read a resume. What you cannot change is *attitude*. Is this person proactive or do they sit around and wait to be told what to do? Are they naturally gregarious? I hate to use the old cliché about the potential team member needing to be a "people person," but it's true. If you aren't genuinely interested in people—their hopes and dreams and vision of the future—you need to be in another line of business.

Of course, you're not running a school for Recruiters. You want professionals who can bring value to your team. Once you have identified a pool of prospects who have the right attitude and team spirit, you can focus on those candidates who can hit the ground running. Let's take a look at some of the attributes that make an outstanding recruiting consultant.

FOCUS ON UNIQUE SKILLS

At a recent panel for the Society for Human Resource Management (SHRM), over 100 thought leaders were asked what skills would be most valued in the HR profession in the future. What would you guess was rated the most important skill? Consultative skills? Yes, important, but no, not the most. Negotiating skills? Key, but not at the top. Executive skills? Sorry.

The single most important skill identified by that group was *Project Management* skills.

"What?" you ask. "Have I just morphed into the section on technical operations?" (Techies are the Project Management kings/queens.)

Nope, you're in the right place.

Now and in the future, a great HR leader will not just do things. The great

HR leaders will be focused on strategic and other key issues of the organization and on building great relationships. They will still be held responsible for everything they're responsible for now; they just won't do it all. Others will do it. That's right—they'll be outsourcing much of it. The great HR executive will come to love outsourcing (if they don't already) the way Marvel's Iron Fist relies on the super power of Jessica Jones. Just as Jessica's talents compliment the Iron Fist's mission, outsourcing will free you up to be the great leaders you always knew you could be. Whether it's using third-party Recruiters, contract Recruiters, recruitment research, outsourced resume mining, background investigations, travel and logistical providers, relocation companies, or recruitment advertising agencies; let's face it, we're moving toward an outsourced world. And that's not a bad thing. It enables you to focus on the core of HR and Talent Acquisition: relationships.

I can hear it now—you're yelling, "What?!? That's my value to the company, what I do. If you get rid of that, I'm afraid of how vulnerable that leaves me."

First of all, you're wrong. Your value to the company is what you make sure gets done, not what you actually do. Second, get over it!

Outsourcing is actually one of the best trends that could happen to our profession. By eliminating the heavy lifting (internet sourcing, resume processing), we can focus on the true value-add of assessing, evaluating, and building a community of top talent for our organizations.

Outsourcing effectively still requires that you have excellent negotiation and candidate development skills, among others. The core of recruiting—your ability to build, develop, and maintain great relationships—cannot be outsourced (North American domestic candidates rarely respond to people calling to recruit them from outsourced recruiting teams overseas). That notwithstanding, you should not spend your time doing high-volume, lower-value work. Others can and should do the resume trolling, the reading of alumni boards, the scanning of social media communities, etc. And let's be honest—as HR executives and Talent Acquisition professionals, we've been outsourcing for years. We may not have called it that, but every time you've ever used a search firm you've outsourced. So, let's not be afraid of it. Let's just do it better. And in order to do it better we need to be great Project Managers.

I know, the first question you have is, "What the heck do ya mean, Project Management? What is Project Management?" Project Management is what Jessica Jones helped the Iron Fist do through her desire to investigate cases when the Iron Fist wanted to forge ahead into battle. She stepped in, took charge, communicated effectively, set boundaries and expectations, and above all, didn't feed his self-destructive behavior (How many clients do we know who are candidate addicts?).

So technically I like to define Project Management as *overseeing, resource leveraging, and facilitating the completion of a temporary endeavor undertaken to achieve a particular aim.*

Now that you've awakened from that boring definition, let me tell you what I think Project Management really is in the world of professional Talent Acquisition:

Facilitating and communicating effectively to ensure a project gets done.

Thus, for Talent Acquisition teams I break Project Management skills/ techniques down in terms of internal versus external projects. In both cases we need to talk about the value of utilizing a contract and "contracting" effectively.

Here are some steps to ensure success:

1. Contracting

In Talent Acquisition we are not in control of the results of our work and so we must contract well. Contracting well is the key to successful Project Management. Internally, this manifests itself in clarifying with a Hiring Manager who is responsible for the end result in the hiring process. The Recruiter plays a key role in this because he/she needs to ask the right questions, make sure to understand the answers, and ensure that the info gathered is correct. The Recruiter should not just take what is said like an order form.

2. Develop a Blueprint/Position Profile

What is needed by the Talent Acquisition professional is an understanding of the scope of the position and the deliverables. What is needed from the Hiring Manager is an honest description of the role. The ultimate goal is a good blueprint in the form of a position specification. The Talent Acquisition manager will need to write something up and give it to the Hiring Manager as a reflection of what was said (this becomes easier once you build up a library of position descriptions; at that point, you can cut and paste, which is what many search firms do).

3. Service Level Agreements

I have seen some use a Service Level Agreement (SLA) to clarify these issues. An SLA is an explicit contract that maps everything out formally. Whether or not that works depends upon an organization's culture. The key is to make sure everyone—the recruiting professional and the Hiring Manager—knows who is responsible for what down the line. The issues to be addressed should include: who will be in charge of scheduling candidates and candidate travel? What will recruiting coordinators do? Who will be their host when they arrive? Who will follow up with candidates? Who will follow up with those in the interview loop? When will the Hiring Manager give feedback (prompt feedback is essential)? Don't actually write up a paper "contract." instead, I recommend sending an e-mail of understanding. It's like a contract but usually more comfortable for all participants and less formal. There are also tools that can help facilitate this process (check out a few examples on RecruitCONSULT.net), however, keeping things simple and spelled out for all parties is the ultimate goal.

4. Working with External Providers

The parameters of working with an external provider for Project Management touch upon many of the same issues as above. However, because they're external, it's even more important that we contract well with them. Many agreements provided by third-party providers don't explicitly lay out who does what in the relationship. There are many assumptions, and with assumptions come issues.

For example, companies assume third-party Recruiters check references before an offer is made or that they (the Recruiters) will sign off on candidates. When they don't, there's trouble. So, if you want things done at a certain time you need to discuss it with the external provider explicitly beforehand and put it in the contract. The point is that the key to your contracting effectively is the quality of the questions you ask and the things you insist get spelled out (remember—Jessica Jones didn't trust the Iron Fist at first and it took some discussion for them both to understand how their power helped their cause!). Because, what you neglect to ask will only hurt you. If candidates are not signed off, they blame the company, not the outside Recruiter. If a research firm only provides you with certain services for their hourly rate (because that's what they provide everyone else) perhaps there's a way to pay them based on results. But how will you know if you don't ask?

Finally, here are the four key things you need to ask to establish an effective contracting relationship, either internally or externally:

1) What needs to be accomplished?

2) Who is responsible for what?

3) How will success or accomplishment be measured?

4) When will we know the task is completed?

Overall, the things you need to contract well include; asking the right questions in advance, figuring out who's responsible for what, timing, and measurements/metrics. Do that and you will become a great Project Manager. You will be able to leverage your time better and focus on strategy and relationships. You will see that outsourcing can be your savior and it will enable you to take superhero strides toward becoming a great HR executive and a thought leader of the future. I have a chapter dedicated to understanding how you might approach getting the best value for your business from outsourcing – you'll get there soon!

We've discussed how to identify a great HR leader and the skills (both the kind you can teach and the kind that are innate) you need to see in a candidate for your team. At the same time you are putting your team together, you will need to consider the optimum structure for your consultative recruiting group. It's a back-and-forth process: the skills of your individual team members may influence the structure of your group, while if you have an existing framework you'll look for people who can fit into it.

STRUCTURING THE TALENT ACQUISITION OPERATION

Fitting in has as much to do with your corporate environment as it does with how the work is divided. You want to avoid encouraging silos within your team while at the same time creating clear division of responsibility. One success factor I have found is the ability to fully "see" your team, meaning is it organized in a way that is easy for you to manage and report on? As a Talent Acquisition leader, if you aren't easily able to produce the proverbial "elevator speech" for your whole team, it is not well designed. A successful Talent Acquisition operation will make it easier for you to continually show value in the areas that matter most to the business—not just HR—as we've discussed.

Depending on the size of the organization, the amount of management within each area may vary, but the following will provide a nice blueprint.

The first area is **Talent Acquisition administration**. I start here because many Talent Acquisition professionals may have been on this team at one point or another in their career. Having the right team in place to manage interview scheduling, generate offer and rejection letters, assist with background investigations and the like will keep your whole Talent Acquisition function running smoothly.

Another area unto itself should be **relationship/account management**. This function bridges to your internal clients (mostly Hiring Managers, but HR types as well). Training and preparation for candidate relations including interview, screening, and overall philosophy is their main responsibility. The idea is to ensure a consistent presentation to the candidate and help build trust so that when issues for discussion arise, such as relocation and immigration, the Talent Acquisition professional is well positioned to make recommendations that are best for the business and that are well received.

Sourcing and candidate relationship management stands alone as well. Having strong internal relationships is important, but equally important are candidate relations, which include work that is candidate-facing, or involves interaction with candidates (both internal and external). Sourcing at the requisition level, candidate screening, and developing dialogue with candidates through social media or talent communities are all responsibilities of this group.

This final area of the structure is for **strategies and programs**. Sometimes called a "Center of Excellence," this part of the team looks at long-term initiatives that support the overall objectives of the team. This happens while all the sourcing, interviewing, scheduling, and training are being done in preparation to fill new roles, to support the additional dimension of expertise the Talent Acquisition team requires. The strategies and programs team develops infrastructure and long-term planning that will enable the other three areas to better execute their roles. The initiatives of this group could include things like; developing diversity programs, building relationships with professional associations and universities, marketing and employment branding, and competitive intelligence research.

The benefit of having a Talent Acquisition operation structured in this way is more than just the preparation of your "elevator speech." It gives your business leaders a better view into what goes into Talent Acquisition and allows you the opportunity to celebrate and recognize the accomplishments of each equally important area. When all four teams are working well together, the transition through the Talent Acquisition process is much smoother and there is less confusion from both Hiring Managers and candidates who each may have several touch points throughout the process.

With clarity and communication this structure should also help create the time to run both the reports that you are interested in and that your business leaders want to see. Your communication can be formal (e.g., an email or newsletter), or informal (e.g., cross-functional meetings), but the objective is for each member of the team to understand the value in working with all areas of Talent Acquisition and to clearly articulate the roles and responsibilities of each functional area. Sometimes it's hard for people to "let go" of the entire picture, but one person couldn't possibly do all four areas independently and provide the consultative, strategic level of service you want to provide. In addition to team-building initiatives, by helping them realize the benefits of focusing on one area and doing it well, you will create a cross-developmental environment that will in turn foster a team of people focused on a career path that is within reach.

CONSULTATIVE STAFFING ORGANIZATION STRUCTURAL MODELS

Like football, where there are a wide range of offensive and defensive formations based on the skills of the players, the strategy of the coach and charasteristics of the opponent will follow the structure of your consultative Talent Acquisition organization. Both will will reflect strategic goals, have human assets, face the weight of management expectations, have budgets, and several other similar factors.

1. Partnership Model

Talent Acquisition and the business are assumed to possess mutually beneficial information needed to facilitate hiring success. Both Talent Acquisition and the business line share accountability for recruiting success. Talent Acquisition is responsible for serving Hiring Managers, but performance is measured against greater organizational goals as well as client satisfaction. Talent Acquisition is responsible for educating Hiring Managers, particularly where business needs/preferences are in conflict with organizational goals. The business pays some variable costs.

Advantages include: recruiting and Hiring Manager's Talent Acquisition goals are aligned around organizational priorities, promoting teamwork and consistency of objectives. In addition, there is the perception that problems and challenges are jointly owned by Talent Acquisition and the business.

Disadvantages include: significant up-front time investment required to establish and maintain a partnership.

2. Center of Excellence/Center-Led Model

In this model, the Chief HR Officer or other organizational head is considered the ultimate "client" of Talent Acquisition. The team's performance is largely measured against corporate goals and Hiring Managers are sometimes viewed with suspicion: They are assumed to not behave in the best interests of the organization or to not possess the "big picture" that Talent Acquisition has access to. Utilization of external recruiting parties is limited and closely monitored. This model works best for university recruiting efforts as well as entry-level jobs that differ little from one business unit to the next (e.g. administrative assistants).

Advantages include: Talent Acquisition has a high degree of visibility among business leaders and their subsequent support, enabling a greater degree of strategic oversight. Talent Acquisition is often "at the table" for executive HR decision meetings. There is an ability to ensure consistency of process across the organization, greater economies of scale, and flexibility to move resources around the organization. The center of excellence/center-led model facilitates compliance and metrics reporting.

Disadvantages include: it can lead to weak relationships with hiring champions because of misalignment of hiring objectives and behaviors. There is a lack of insight into line concerns and perspectives, and there is a tendency to be more operationally focused than customer/consultative focused.

3. Client/Vendor Model

Typically found in highly decentralized organizations, in the client/vendor model Hiring Managers have the option to use external recruiting vendors as an alternative to internal recruiting. It is an SLA-driven culture and recruiting charges some services back to the line. Talent Acquisition "value" and performance objectives are defined by the line and measurement of recruiting performance is based largely on client satisfaction. This model is sometimes a consequence of a poor record of recruiting service.

Advantages include: Emphasis on SLAs and client service creates a high degree of accountability for Talent Acquisition. Response times are fast and the chargeback structure gives line transparency into costs, motivating "good" Hiring Manager behaviors (such as greater commitment to retention). Talent Acquisition also develops close relationships with the line and deep knowledge of line needs.

Disadvantages include: lack of insight into broader organizational goals ("the big picture"). A lack of leverage can rob Talent Acquisition of its ability to drive organizational goals, eliminate redundancies, and promote consistency of process. It sometimes lacks economies of scale and has inconsistent or redundant processes that can lead to competition for the same candidates. There is no centralized metrics reporting, no best practices sharing, and possible legal exposure.

4. Full-Cycle Talent Acquisition Model

Talent Acquisition professionals are typically responsible for all parts of recruitment assessment, offer/declination, and other duties. This model is typically organized by client group (line of business or department or division), functional (operations, sales/commercial, finance, and so on across multiple lines of business), or geographic (where teams recruit along regional alignment).

Advantages include: resource flexibility (can move Talent Acquisition professionals around the organization if demand shifts). Talent Acquisition professionals typically like this model because they get to do "everything." They have control and visibility, and there is usually very high-quality client engagement.

Disadvantages include: sourcing, candidate development, and pipeline recruiting are typically poor in this model. It is less likely to have specialists on the team and if it is not organized around function there can be cannibalization (all recruiting teams drawing from same pools). There is little expertise or organizational knowledge gained; lessons and best practices cycle through with staff. Having more silo recruiting teams equals less sharing of candidates, less economy of scale (vendors), and inconsistency in brand messaging and process. Finally, it's tough to scale.

5. Central Sourcing Model

This model is characterized by separation by sub-function, typically into "relationship management" and "sourcers." Relationship management Recruiters focus on Hiring Manager and finalist candidate relationships while sourcer Recruiters focus on candidate generation and candidate development. Relationship management Recruiters are aligned by function, client group, or geography whereas sourcing Recruiters work as a team in a central, shared service environment. Relationship management Recruiters access sourcing services as needed. Sourcing Recruiters typically do not have relationships with the business line.

Advantages include: better candidate pipelines and external sourcing activities that allow for faster time to interview. There is flexible and more variable Talent Acquisition of the centralized sourcing Recruiters (as volumes change, the central team can change). Greater sourcing expertise can be developed by centralizing and focusing sourcing as a single team.

Disadvantages include: a vendor/client situation is set up between Talent Acquisition teams and often becomes negative. Territorial issues are commonplace and relationship management Recruiters often lose touch with external candidate pools. Sourcer Recruiters are often demotivated by the lack of exposure to the results of recruiting efforts and lack of exposure to the hiring champions and final candidates.

6. Distributed Sourcing Model

In this model Talent Acquisition professionals are grouped together in clusters or "pods" aligned by function, client group, or geography. Relationship management Recruiters, sourcing Recruiters, and administrative/logistical support coordinators work together as a team to recruit for their assigned alignment. Relationship management Recruiters and sourcing Recruiters are peers (not client/vendor to each other), and team members work together to achieve the goals for Talent Acquisition, including being measured by the same metrics. Often clusters/pods are arranged by physically having team members housed in the same area.

Advantages include: it allows for the ability to build strong pipelines and new candidate streams. It builds solid team orientation amongst cluster/pod team members and provides dedicated team support to hiring champion teams (appears to have a team rather than an individual service their needs). It also allows for cross training and development across types of roles (i.e., relationship management Recruiter can develop sourcing Recruiters, and vice versa), allowing for flexibility of Talent Acquisition levels.

Disadvantages include: difficulty in initially setting up the clusters/pods with the right team members that work together. It can be difficult to change or flex staff because of alignment of function, client group, or geography. In organizations with multiple clusters or pods, it can be difficult to ensure limits on cannibalization of candidate pools.

7. Functionally Aligned Model

In this model, there are several advantages. Recruiters develop job and marketplace knowledge and skill specialization and form deeper relationships within the candidate communities. Recruiters can more easily offer candidates multiple opportunities within their job category, leveraging a candidate's preferences to increase the chances of making the hire (e.g., give them the shift and location they want). It's easier to share candidates within a central, functional team than across businesses and easier to measure critical recruiting strategies and share best practices among Recruiters. The functional Talent Acquisition leader can realign people easily based on priorities and changes within the portfolios. He or she can also cover Recruiters' away time (during vacations or career fairs), leverage recruiting strategies optimized for the whole organization, and respond to changes in volume of recruiting needs. It is easier to establish the tools, processes, and methodologies that Recruiters will use to do their jobs when centrally organized. This includes training Recruiters and helping them develop new skills.

Disadvantages include: business does not have its own dedicated Talent Acquisition team that it can realign and control as its Talent Acquisition needs change. Some Hiring Managers may interact with different Recruiters for similar jobs. A strong Talent Acquisition leader will be required: they will lead a larger central team, and it can be difficult to find subject matter expertise with strong leadership skills in a competitive market. It may be harder for the Recruiters to develop deep content knowledge about each of the portfolios and the unique needs of HR and Hiring Managers within those businesses.

8. Business-Unit Aligned Model

This model also offers several advantages including: the package of a one-stop shop because there are fewer points of contact for the Hiring Manager. Team focus means HR Generalists and Recruiters work closely together with a specific business-unit focus. HR leadership team can prioritize Talent Acquisition focus within their groups and process and reporting can be customized to business leadership. Communication may be better between HR and Talent Acquisition even as there is more autonomy to launch small-scale Talent Acquisition efforts.

Disadvantages include: all Recruiters—across businesses—are drawing from the same pools, creating many more opportunities for duplicate candidate contact. There are more silos within the Talent Acquisition team, less sharing of candidates, and less economies of scale.

This leads to less specialization for Recruiters as they'll potentially be spread thin across more job types and not able to establish deeper networks within each job category. More Recruiters may be needed to cover all job categories and good Recruiters are in high demand. It is harder to leverage functional, enterprise-wide strategies. More Recruiters need to be involved in career fairs as it is harder to divvy up candidates that come in from sources like nationwide ads.

RECRUITER MANAGEMENT

We've all seen the challenge with "superstars" at other companies coming into a new environment and not having the same success. Some people are surprised by this, but the bottom line is—like with best practices—no two companies, candidates, teams, or anything else will ever be identical, and what worked in the past won't universally work in the future.

The bottom line seems to be skills and specializations. What made the person a "superstar" in a previous role, and how can those competencies be incorporated into the team to add additional value? Perhaps it has to do with the type of relationships they excel at developing or their ability to conduct research. It could even be their interest in metrics or marketing.

Whether the person has been staffing-specific or owns a part of Talent Acquisition through their HR Generalist role, there will be common competencies and performance traits that are common to both. A "Recruiter Competency Model" can look at several traits each Talent Acquisition professional should possess: core Talent Acquisition skills, innate performance traits, and executive search and partnership competencies. We'll get back to these in more detail, but first think about the skills available on the team versus the services and consultation you will need to provide. Do you have a big enough bench strength? If not, can you train and upskill? Can the current team change focus and be successful over a period if required (i.e., from managing projects, to full-time sourcing, to strategic planning)?

With the questions you just answered, think about the traits of your own Recruiter Competency Model.

Do your team members have **core recruiting skills**, the ones that often tell you this person likes what they do, enjoys meeting people, and carries a curious streak that helps them establish if "good on paper" translates to a good fit? These skills have to do with the ability to assess, summarize, interact, sell, and close an offer.

Do your team members have the innate **performance traits**, the ones that will energize the whole team because they are so passionate about finding the right candidates? Are they willing to go that extra mile to make both the candidate, and internal stakeholders happy? These skills are often very customer-aligned. They will be innovative and have the flexibility to change course when needed because it is all about the experience.

Do your team members have a business savvy approach that would lead to success with **executive search and partnership competencies?** These skills often surface as a genuine interest in the business and where the industry is going as a whole, not just Talent Acquisition. This intelligence to understand their business, in addition to their role, often makes them quite organized and good leaders because they are excellent relationship builders and expert networkers.

We often get off track when we interview, hire, and then realize there is not a good match. If your sourcing is in desperate need of attention and you don't end up with someone with good performance traits who is willing to stick to the task until it is operating at full capacity, the whole team is impacted.

Let's pause for a moment and do a visualization exercise. Think of the most difficult relationship you have within the business, or the hardest role to fill, or the team that has seen the most change in the shortest amount of time. Is the Recruiter in front of you going to be able to find solutions and add value to each of these scenarios? Will they be motivated and able to do it confidently and approach it with a repeatable methodology that can be rolled out to the rest of the team? Can they handle the pressure of timelines, executives looking for answers, and managing multiple high-priority projects?

If they can do all this, now think about the individual themselves. Where are they in their career and how soon will they want more/less responsibility, accountability, or autonomy, and will you able to provide it to them in the current environment? Will they be able to fit into the environment? Can they handle some of the lengthier processes, unavoidable administration, and red tape every organization has in varying quantities? Each individual has their own tolerance level and there is only so much you can control about the role, the office environment, and the interpersonal relationships that will form. As a Talent Acquisition leader, you should keep a pulse on these controllable areas for ongoing evaluation. It all comes down to engagement. Engaged employees are more productive, motivated, and interested in the success of the business and contributing to that success.

In the area of Talent Acquisition, the *motivators* of top performing Recruiters will often include being closer to the business, building direct relationships with business leaders, and understanding the needs of these leaders. If they are motivated to take the initiative on these areas it will later benefit the Talent Acquisition leader as well, who will have more information to gather for their 360-degree review and for recognition purposes.

On the other side of the scale, there are factors that will *demotivate* Recruiters as well, and awareness is the first step in prevention. The most frequent challenge I hear from Recruiters is the access barriers to the business, whether this is because they are snowed over with administration or because the hierarchy of the organization traditionally doesn't allow for it. It creates a feeling of recruiting at an arm's length and reduces recognition for their work as candidates are closed. Closing candidates is another motivator, so when the employment offers that are approved are not that easily "sellable" on an industry scale, it creates a very quick downer.

When managing Recruiters, location is an important factor as well – regardless of which Talent Acquisition model you use. I've had many clients who have attempted to successful fully remote teams and have failed. This can be for many reasons, for example, the business itself does not operate remotely, or is vastly spread out and your team cannot be co-located in every office. There is a logical flow for some groups, for example, if your full business is used to working remotely, like sales or operations groups, or if the business is geographically disparate, then a remote Talent Acquisition function makes sense and is possible.

When you have a centralized business or even a singular place of business, allowing and planning for remote workers becomes much harder to do. As this is a popular topic I am approached about, I'll give a few examples on how to manage Recruiters from a distance, and go a little deeper on the instances where success is more likely.

Companies with lots of plants, those in the retail or hospitality industries will often have a large field and regional population. These employees and business leaders are used to speaking with people who are not right in front of them. In these scenarios, you have more choice on getting the top talent, not only for your team, but for your organization as you're not limited by one location. The best Recruiters may not be located in your city, and have strong track records of success being mostly on the phone or online. As long as there is no expectation that these Recruiters will meet all candidates in person, they can be effective in phone screens and recommending candidates to proceed to meet with Hiring Managers from anywhere. At times, remote employees can also be effective in a 'follow the sun' approach whereby coordinating with a shared services team in other time zones so you have continuous coverage.

If you work at an organization that is remote-friendly, then you can highly endorse having your team remote as well. It will help you get the best talent. Do keep these caveats and tips in mind though in terms of your ability to effectively manage remote employees, even if they are high performing;

1. Ensure the SLA and expectations from the business align with a remote approach. If they do, be clear about the location and in-person availability of your Recruiters.

2. Plan for extra travel budget to ensure you can meet face-to-face with your team and they can spend time with others on the team. This should be budgeted for at least a few visits each year.

3. Plan extra time for these employees, including dedicated time for both training, relationship building, and team building activities. Having people work in isolation over the long haul is a recipe for immediate failure.

4. Budget your own time. It's vital that you have video chats and weekly connection points with these employees. Skip one and you could very quickly see them lose touch with the team's processes, mission, and vibe.

I had a client who makes consumer products. Their sales team was all remote, so they decided all Recruiters would be too. The challenge with this company was that one of their products was focused on dental hygiene, so part of the candidate screening process included seeing the candidate's teeth. While they used video chat, it was not always effective, and they were forced to move to a model whereby Recruiters had to meet candidates in person.

I had another client who was in the health and wellness industry and similar to retail or hospitality, their employees needed to reflect their brand. While discriminatory, it was an important part of their image, and past success. It is important for some businesses to see their candidates, and in some instances, technology can help overcome this criteria.

Video interviewing is an effective way to manage a team that is completely virtual. They can also invest time in outbound videos, for example Hiring Managers can send video job descriptions or posting, to get crisp on what they are looking for, or can record questions that can be scored after interviews are complete.

One of our manufacturer clients has their headquarters in Athens, Greece and operates in 28 countries in Europe. They also have operations in Nigeria – and each function as local operations. Their Talent Acquisition network of teams is supported by a shared services team in another country. They don't see each other and only communicate over phone and email. Once a year, they spend a lot of money to bring all together for a week. The team receives a few days of training and process updates and they reserve one day for team building activities that the team views favorably and creates enough engagement momentum to carry this team for another year.

Virtual teams require leadership. This is not a good place to slip or get lazy because it isolates your team quickly. Even if you set up a virtual buddy or mentor for these team members, they must maintain contact with you and their internal stakeholders.

Personally, I believe that Talent Acquisition teams, leaders, Recruiters, and Sourcers can work remotely and it is totally fine. You must work really hard to engage with the team and the business. Double your efforts if the business is not generally set up for a remote employee experience and watch carefully for any pitfalls and early lack of engagement.

WHAT DO THE BEST TALENT ACQUISITION RELATIONSHIP MANAGERS (RECRUITERS) DO?

Relationships are hard and even the best aren't always on point. Relationships are an ongoing, growing, and quickly changing element of business that impact how well you will be able to do your role and keep things moving.

When looking at the role of "Talent Acquisition relationship managers" (Recruiters) it's sometimes easier to take it outside the office first with a list of "don'ts." This may come from a family member, partner, or spouse, but regardless of the source, have a look at this list of how to "kill" a relationship.

1. **Don't dance, in general, and especially if you have two left feet.** If you have something to say or are asked a direct question, don't waste time dancing around it. If you dance or avoid admitting you're wrong, learn from the experience and move on.

2. **Don't hide behind technology.** There are so many ways to "connect" without ever truly connecting, so make the effort to be present and spend time in person. Then you will know the relationship is as strong as it can be.

3. **Don't believe that silence is golden. Has it ever really been?** Whether it's your mother wondering why you haven't called in a week or your friends wondering why you haven't updated your social media if you're an active poster, always provide an update, even if it's to say there is no update. There is always some sort of progress that you can share and let people know you are alive, well, and productive.

4. **Don't think too much.** Yes, of course you need to think, but be cognizant of how often you start your interactions with "I think." It doesn't sound very confident if you never "know" or "feel sure," and it's hard to be viewed as a credible source if you're always just "thinking."

5. **Don't rely exclusively on experience.** Part of building the credibility you have comes from your track record and examples you share, research you've done, measurement, and your ability to argue against bad ideas to save people from making less than ideal decisions.

6. **Don't assume, as this gets us into trouble far too often.** When you show up three hours late at your partner's lecture series because you didn't follow up to confirm the time, it's never a good situation. Rather than assuming and relying on your memory, send follow-up e-mails that outline what was agreed on and keep the trail!

7. **Don't just talk.** Active listening is becoming a more and more sought after skill, especially as things change so quickly. When you listen, you learn what is most important to the person you're speaking with, where the value in responding is, and explicit and inferred timelines.

8. **Don't forget to give credit where it's due.** If something has been accomplished, send a card or write a positive e-mail (in the workplace this could be a Hiring Manager learning your process and becoming the ideal Recruiter partner and brand champion for candidates).

9. **Don't come to the party with dark clouds over your head.** Be positive and solution-oriented if there is a problem and offer recommendations for people to think about. "No! No! No!" isn't what anyone wants to hear.

CREATING THE RecruitCONSULT! CULTURE

Consultative Talent Acquisition is not just an idea or concept or brand. It's about Recruiters actively partnering with the client (the Hiring Manager) on strategy, approach, and problems/challenge. It's about helping the business without becoming a customer service Recruiter. It's essentially "teaching them to fish."

It's about aligning activities to business priorities and demonstrating their alignment.

Demonstrate your expertise (be credible) via your language, your metrics/reports, your communication of wins/losses, and your personal priorities. Push back on bad ideas. But we must be willing to back down if we have made our point and it is not accepted.

We are not "customer service," we are consultants. We must view ourselves and our peers as experts in our area of specialization. We must convey that expertise through deeds and actions, not just by saying so.

We must stay on top of our profession and trends. Allow your Recruiters to do the same and let them show their capability. Your role as their leader is to coach and mentor.

CONCLUSION

In this chapter we've seen that assembling your consultative Talent Acquisition team using the RecruitCONSULT! philosophy is not unlike putting together a sports team. You need to find the most highly skilled players who have the drive to win and the willingness to set egos aside to reach the common goal.

While professional experience is good, it's not just about technical skills, which can be acquired. It's also about innate qualities: the desire to bring value, to win, to think creatively, and to know how to bring out the best in people.

As a consultative Talent Acquisition leader, you need to lead by example. The same attributes that you seek in a Recruiter are the ones that your client seeks in you. When this is all put together you have a consultative culture that works as one harmonious whole, always moving fearlessly forward.

CHAPTER 6: LEADING A PROACTIVE TALENT ACQUISITION FUNCTION

In any consultative Talent Acquisition organization your product is people. You can't create them; either you need to find them or they need to find you. The ones whom you seek out and contact are not necessarily looking for a career change—they are passive. The ones who are openly looking for a career or a new job are active. The successful consultative corporate Talent Acquisition function that leverages the RecruitCONSULT! philosophy will engage in a mix of strategies and activities to recruit both the passive candidates and the active candidates.

Active and Passive Recruiting

The way you plan for your sourcing depends on how you will find the active and passive candidates because these two categories of candidates are found using different methods.

- **Active candidates** are those in the candidate pool who are actively applying to your company and are actively seeking you out.

- **Passive candidates** are not actively seeking you or your company out, but, depending upon how passive they are, they may be "found."

Many Talent Acquisition professionals tend to think that passive candidates are too hard to find using lower-cost methods. Not all passive candidate sources are expensive.

Prospects Who Are Actively Looking Are Visible Through:
- Job fairs/open houses

- Employee referrals

People Who Are Passively Looking May Be Visible Here:
- Internet job board postings

- Resume database mining

- Employee referrals

- Social networking sites (such as LinkedIn, Facebook, and Twitter) internet job board postings and other advertising

- Our own career pages and candidate communities

- Resume database mining

- Outplacement resources

People Who Are Not Looking May Be Visible Here:
- Direct sourcing and networking

- Community outreach (community-based organizations, religious organizations)

- Employee referrals

- Internet mining

- Direct e-mail/mail

- Associations

- Trade shows/conventions

- Social networking sites

There are many recruiting teams that "post and pray"—the teams post a job on an online job board and pray that the right people apply. No one will apply who is not actively looking. That is not recruiting, although the resulting active candidates often turn out to be perfectly acceptable. However, leaders must ensure that Recruiters are leveraging both active candidates and passive candidates who are not looking for a job and have to be found or headhunted.

THE BALANCE BETWEEN ACTIVE AND PASSIVE RECRUITING

I once heard a story about a CEO of a major executive search firm who told a group of newly minted partners never to present candidates who are unemployed. When one of the new partners raised his hand and challenged the CEO on how the firm could adequately serve its clients without evaluating all potential candidates, the CEO implied that, by definition, anyone who is unemployed is inferior.

I understand this line of thinking. It's simple, concise, and easy to categorize. A "sexy" pitch. In fact, it's the same line of thinking that leads to the idea that anyone who hangs out with a communist must be a communist sympathizer.

In short, it's dead wrong.

It is incendiary, irresponsible, and extremely one-sided. And it's not like I believe the opposite line of thinking to be true either (that all recruiting should be focused on those who are unemployed). Quite the contrary. I have a problem with that version as well.

I've read a number of articles and other content by recruiting "influencers" implying (or even overtly stating) that passive recruiting is a "shameful practice" and contributes to the distrust of the corporate world by the many millions of workers who are seeking employment. Passive recruiting shameful? Again, this reasoning is as misguided as the CEO above.

To suggest that passive recruiting – whether the economy is stable or a little less than optimal – is unethical is a misnomer that fails to take into account the bigger picture. It is true that most industries see numerous applicants per position, but for many companies, these numbers do not equate to larger pools of *qualified* candidates. Instead it creates an additional burden for lean HR teams as they spend more time processing unqualified applicants. The fact of the matter is successful companies use the most cost-effective means to recruit qualified candidates, whether it is a direct hire or a passive candidate.

Recruiters want to fill the job perhaps more than anyone. If the requisition has attracted what appear to be top candidates, they look no further. If not, they need to source.

When it comes to recruiting, one size does *not* fit all. Great recruiting requires both active and passive strategies and, in short, good, hard work. As with most things, to review in terms of extremes doesn't add value to the situation. For instance, the idea that active recruiting involves "damaged goods" is simply not always the case—and it takes a great HR person to know the difference.

There is no denying that many share the opinion that the best people don't get laid off. But this is a narrow point of view; situations certainly exist that put even the best people at risk. It's important to be open to all candidates. A great

Recruiter's sourcing involves multiple activities to find the perfect candidate. Professional networking tools are used, and it's important to consider that Recruiters often can't really tell if someone is still employed or not because people are not updating their profiles when they first leave a job. They sometimes wait so they don't appear to be unemployed, or for other various reasons. Since this is a candidate-owned portal, they will present the story they want you to see.

To be sure, there are candidates who have been laid off for performance reasons, and companies do use economic downturns to mask laying off people for those issues. Companies know there are a lot more active candidates in the marketplace and thus they can replace the individual laid off quicker. So, while there are certainly individuals with professional red flags in the marketplace, the successful Recruiter will have a balanced view that enables them to sort through all candidates.

There are undoubtedly specific roles where the chances are 90% or more of appropriate candidates will be developed through passive recruiting. For certain roles, in certain professions, there are simply not a lot of candidates and the best people are employed elsewhere. While recruiting passive candidates is very costly, it is essential in industries that have large barriers to entry and, as a result, smaller qualified applicant pools.

Those in the health care industry know this quite well. Health care organizations tend to be specific in what they are looking for and the requirements are often dictated by government bodies and accrediting organizations. After all, doctors and nurses need to have a valid license.

Thus, if you're a company looking for these types of people you have to know where they are and be able to convince them to come elsewhere. To not adopt this approach for these key roles would be corporately irresponsible.

But a vital element in all of this is you don't have to pursue only one strategy. The different approaches do require different skill sets. Active candidate Recruiters tend to have a "post and pray" mentality and are very assessment-focused, while passive candidate Recruiters are skilled at sourcing strategy and research, among other things.

The key is that as Recruiters and HR professionals, we have to develop skills and techniques to do both and should not necessarily be single-strategy focused. Some (dare I say many) roles will require both an assessment and sourcing strategy. For example, data mining to buy a list of people in a geographical area to see who has a nursing license and find all qualified nursing candidates, even those not working in a traditional setting today?

It is incumbent upon Talent Acquisition professionals to design and pursue strategies to find the best talent quickly. In a high unemployment market, it is true that there are more active candidates; however, this does not mean that Recruiters can become complacent and rely upon one source. Posting a job so that active candidates may apply is not a silver bullet. What if the right candidate does not apply? A good Recruiter will focus on attracting active applicants and, in parallel, search for passive candidates.

However, a question bigger than all of this lurks: as Talent Acquisition teams have dwindled in companies and the Recruiting Specialists have left, where do we go to identify candidates?

The answer, as you may have guessed, turns out to be not one but *many* places. They include everything from utilizing outsourced providers to developing appropriate sourcing methods in-house, as mentioned above.

Ultimately, companies and Recruiters are striving to do the right thing, which is create jobs and help keep the unemployment rate low. Take the U.S. market, for example. If the national jobless rate is 8% or 9%, this means that 80% or 90% of Americans are employed. No line manager or company playing to win in this economy would say they want to ignore 90% of the potential talent. Put another way, who would only want to consider 10% of the possible candidates? The right thing, while it may not seem obvious to all, is to consider all candidates, whether they are active, or passive.

If your ultimate goal is to increase your value to your organization and be the best Talent Acquisition function possible, you have to stay away from an all-or-nothing mentality. In the end, in tight economic situations, it may get you nothing.

When crafting your consultative Talent Acquisition strategy—especially if you're on a tight budget—you may wonder if active or passive recruiting is inherently more costly than the other. The fact is that there are effective, low-cost strategies that cover both active and passive campaigns.

LOW-COST/NO-COST RECRUITING AND TALENT ACQUISITION TECHNIQUES

Recruiting can be challenging, especially in a down economy, because employed people don't want to make a move (it's risky), and there are far more candidates on the market to sift through than in better economic times. It is important for consultative Talent Acquisition professionals to understand how to plan a Talent Acquisition strategy when there is a need, and to decide what the sourcing process will be prior to actually having to do it.

What is a Talent Acquisition Strategy?

A Talent Acquisition strategy is the result of consultative work with business leaders, Hiring Managers, and your HR partners that leads you to an agreed-upon plan of action to hire the skills you need. It generally involves budget forecasting and an element of budget management and drives the actions (and spending) of the Talent Acquisition team.

The formation of the Talent Acquisition strategy starts well before the Hiring Manager intake process when there is an open position. We talked about what motivates Recruiters earlier and one of the motivators is access and a good relationship with business leaders. In order to establish this, the recruiting professionals need to think like a **STAR.**

Strategy
Recruiting professionals should know it intimately so that there is a consistent approach. This may even involve developing a toolkit when introducing the strategy to the Recruiters so they can use these for intake meetings.

Treatment
What kind of treatment are the Hiring Managers experiencing? They need to be thinking "white glove" treatment all the way. This means everything the Hiring Manager could possibly want (from recommendation on university programs that will train for a skill set required in the future, to compensation packages for similar positions) and bringing it to the meeting. Treating stakeholders in a professional, prepared manner builds the relationship and saves time. It also will likely improve the treatment the Recruiters get in return.

Amaze
If you've made the team aware of the strategy and they have earned credibility through the treatment they have given, they will be in a great position to amaze by doing some pre-sourcing. For example, bringing some resumes that fit the requisition or job demonstrates an understanding of the Hiring Manager's needs. This not only saves money, but it will also help with your internal brand (more on this topic coming soon), which is a way to amaze.

Recruit
Now that you're confident you're on the right track and have provided a consultative approach, it's time to get tactical. Get to it, always keeping your strategy in mind.

If you are able to have your Recruiters join the **STAR** status, next you'll want to look at your specific tactics. Here are some low-cost/no-cost sourcing channels that could be considered as part of a Talent Acquisition strategy:

Referrals
Employee referrals (ER) are the number one source of candidates by far—and usually rated the best quality source. ER programs don't always

have to have a monetary reward, though many do, and the best focus on recognition and simplicity.

Recognizing employees for their referral quickly is the key. Instead of monetary rewards, think about other less costly rewards that focus on the recognition.

Teach your employees how to make great referrals. Ask specific employees about specific jobs; don't just create and publicize the program. HR pros must proactively manage ER so don't put too many rules or barriers to participate in the process. Recognize referrals immediately and follow up on referrals to ensure success. If you pay a reward, consider paying it immediately upon hire and consider alternative ways to pay including branded debit cards and check ceremonies. If your team has current or past candidates that are already in your database ask them about not only their interest but also if they have referrals. Every time you have an opportunity to make a reference call ask the reference contact about referrals. And consider building a reference spreadsheet to share contacted references with the team for use in future searches.

Job Boards

Job boards are great for attracting active candidates. Ensure that your team's postings are well written from a candidate's "what's in it for me" perspective. Don't use company acronyms and slang. Check out and "borrow" great postings using the job board's search system. Make sure your posting is easily findable and is refreshed regularly. Resume databases are quite expensive, and because of this, I don't usually suggest them if we are focusing on low-cost resources. However, there are some other alternatives to this option including the use of free or "niche" job boards.

Social Networking

Social networks provide a great opportunity to find more passive candidates. Using social networks only help your Recruiters *find possible targets to contact*—you still have to call or contact these people! Keep this in mind when you are planning your recruitment strategy. Since your time is limited, focus on the best resources:

LinkedIn

First, make sure your team members are easily found. Make sure their profiles are complete and they have filled in summaries and descriptions well. Make sure profiles are "public." Change the settings in LinkedIn to ensure that they are findable in Google. There are places on profiles to include links to websites for your company and other information. Your team should thoughtfully ask and answer questions in LinkedIn answers to be more findable.

Use LinkedIn Groups to join and start groups, and you can actually post jobs here for free! Use the LinkedIn search tools to find targets. Invite people who are able to expand your network to find the type of people you want (like your Hiring Managers). I usually use these LinkedIn sources to build a call list to actually call or e-mail them directly (outside of LinkedIn). LinkedIn "InMail" is limited and more expensive.

Facebook

Facebook is still targeted at a slightly younger audience. It's harder to find sources on Facebook, but your team can use regular searches to find their co-workers, classmates, and others to get beyond their own network. Search for Friends on Facebook, or leverage it to find candidates to join Facebook pages that are appropriate to you and your jobs. Facebook company pages are also great ways to attract candidates.

Twitter

It is even harder to find people on Twitter, but most tweets are public and searchable. Use Twitter to broadcast your jobs to relevant people or talk about your company's culture.

Blogs

Search relevant online blogs for subject matter experts and sources of candidate referrals. Find blogs by using Google Blog search, and review the "about me" section. Look at their blogroll to find others who share the same interest. Discussion groups are great places to search too—you can simply review their content and decide if you want to pursue.

Google

Googling for candidates is an even more specialized skill, one that is free, provided the Recruiter has the skill to do it well. There are great resources out there to learn how to do this even more effectively.

The lowest cost solution may not always be the best resource to actually save money. Consider alternatives to full-priced recruitment outsourcing and search firms.

Resume Mining Services

Instead of buying expensive resume database access, consider using a "Resume Mining Service." These services offer a low-cost solution on a per-job basis or in packages of jobs. The work they do is simple: they source and scour online resume databases for actual resumes and provide those resumes to you, usually overnight. Most services can offer an additional resource to do quick telephone screens on the resumes submitted.

Recruitment research outsources the cold calling, candidate identification (the "finding"), and candidate development (turning cold calls into candidates that may be interested in your job). You own all of the information provided and you typically pay for the time spent, not on a hire. This is a great resource for harder to find, higher-level roles.

Nontraditional Search and Recruitment Outsourcing Services

Some search firm providers will now price their fees to be more flexible and affordable.

- "Contingency" means that you pay a fee (traditionally about 20-30% of the first year's total cash compensation) only after the hire is made.

- "Retained" means that you pay a fee (traditionally about 30-35% of the first year's total cash compensation, plus expenses) for the professional services related to that search whether you make a hire or not.

- Flexible searches can now include the idea of "retingency" or "container" fees, which would involve paying some form of retainer and then, if a hire is made, a contingency fee as well.

- Search firms can also unbundle their services (research, candidate development, interviewing and assessment, referencing).

MISTAKES TO AVOID

Here are some common pitfalls that your Recruiters don't want to fall into.

Sourcing or Harvesting

Some companies are confusing *proactive talent sourcing* with the simple *harvesting* of resumes from job boards. The former can become the basis of relationship-building with budding leaders in targeted functions and organizations. The latter is just a lot of data about job-seekers—some of whom can be outstanding candidates, but not always.

Some large companies do this because it's easy and inexpensive and because they think the market is loaded with available talent right now. These companies get what they pay for.

What's really bad is that some executive search firms also rely on these methods and resources.

Missing the Audience

In recruiting, the target audience matters as much as it does in marketing. Your job descriptions or candidate profiles need to align to your business' diverse needs for talent. If top candidates read a description that doesn't connect in any way, essentially not saying 'me' on it, you're losing a competitive advantage. I recommend looking at your audience as part of a channel marketing strategy. You can ensure the outreach sounds relevant to the audience and measure using the tools, technology and analytics outlined earlier in the book. In this area, use your data to attempt to communicate with the audience by showing them things that will make them seem comfortable.

Preferential Providers

Many retained search firms, particularly boutiques and niche players, are more interested in partnering with clients these days, but the large global search firms may be more rigid and less willing to be creative. They have resisted, for example, making part of the fee contingent on success.

Preferred provider programs continue to be popular but are therefore more difficult to manage. They work best for companies that do not promise search work to selected firms but offer them opportunities to make bids for appropriate engagements.

Unconscious Biases

Make sure you're not talking, seeing or interacting with an unconscious bias. As a Talent Acquisition leader, you have to work at training, coaching, mentoring your team. If you don't address it, you're not dealing with the issue – be direct. People don't realize that they tend to hire people like them, or already in the group they are recruiting for. As a Recruiter, I caught myself hiring for accounting, and I knew 12 other people, all a certain type of person. They were generally run by white men, most staff were referrals, any time there was an opening, they would bring their friends through – as a Recruiter, I thought someone else wouldn't fit on the team, so didn't consider them if they weren't very similar to the team members we already had.

The challenge is that fit based on existing environment, or following a "Bro Code" doesn't make the organization better. We need to hire for cultural fitness in the future and not looking to maintain what we have today for as long as we can. People can conform, adapt, and enmesh into the culture even if they haven't worked in your specific environment before – it *does not* mean that they can't. When I was the leader of the function, we'd have our team meetings, and bring everyone together. One tactic I used was to facilitate a quick topic conversation on unconscious bias and ask each member of the team to talk about a situation they caught themselves having an unconscious bias. If they didn't have an example, I'd share one. It was important to make sure we had an opportunity to share a time we caught ourselves – and have it out in the open for Recruiters. If you invest in coaching and mentoring on this in an open way with consistency in how you approach avoiding biases, simply the cognition will improve your ability to be successful.

CONCLUSION

In this chapter I tackled some of the nuts and bolts of running your consultative Talent Acquisition group. To fill any given position, either now or in the future, your pool of candidates should include both passive candidates who are not looking for a new job and candidates who are actively looking. Since nearly every Talent Acquisition group must operate under budget constraints, I reviewed the most effective low-cost strategies for reaching out to both passive and active candidates. While you are responsible for the full function, there are times when it makes sense to outsource more of the actual work – let's look deeper into this in the next chapter.

CHAPTER 7: RECRUITMENT PROCESS OUTSOURCING

In the introduction of the book, I talked about the struggle I had in wanting to do everything myself. I wanted my team to be the hero, and that initially meant keeping every process close to me. Well, as we know, that is not always the right solution. The other side of the coin is not always the right answer either—as the real, and perceived, <u>expense</u> of doing everything through Recruitment Process Outsourcing (RPO).

"I'm in the business of losing money."

"I love to spend more than I have to."

"Given the choice, I would pay more for a lower quality of service".

These are statements you will *never* hear from your executive team, and ones that would never cross your mind. It's because they are not conducive to running a profitable business. And yet, many Talent Acquisition leaders inherit or try to over-outsource their business.

I am very supportive of strategically using small or medium RPO firms for the Talent Acquisition functions that are outside of the core of your business. As for the end-to-end large global RPO providers, I'll provide some data points for you to consider as to why some of those firms are not the panacea many see it as.

If you have identified the types of jobs that are most critical to your business – for example the ones that develop your product, and the ones that get your product into the hands of your customers – then you are clear on where you make money. Your team needs to own these and the core functions of bringing this talent into the organization. I strongly suggest not outsourcing your 'mojo' – the thing you work so hard at to show your team is a strategic partner to the business. It may seem better, cheaper and faster at the beginning, but it is actually not the case.

HOW RPO WORKS

I've heard a lot of speculation about the idea of Business Process Out-sourcing (BPO) for transactional work. The rise of BPO has brought forth a lot of curiosity and support around the use of RPO for Recruiting. RPO firms have been selling a value proposition of lower costs and better service through their process. What is often learned later is that over time, the ideals and the promise of some RPO providers are not always delivered. Some RPO implementations are far better and more successful than others and in my opinion and experience, the ones that are successful remove the transactional elements of the recruiting process, but overall recognize that recruiting is not a transactional activity. Recruiting overall is a core business process that when implemented effectively, allows organizations to improve performance and gain a competitive advantage to 'win' against competitors. It means that building a strong recruiting function is essential, whether it's done internally or externally.

With flashy marketing campaigns and benefits that are financially attrac-tive to CFOs and CHROs, many large RPO firms have figured out processes and systems to make money across multiple clients. Many of them sell it by leaning heavily on the notion that they remove cost from your planned budget, which will save you money on your headcount. We can all agree this is a closely monitored cost in many organizations.

Regardless of the type of company or industry, and whether it's a public or private entity, headcount in the General Administration (GA) line where HR sits, is highly scrutinized. If you have 60 jobs that can be outsourced to create a variable cost, this is generally seen as a positive thing to do. What tends to happen though, is that many large RPO firms use talented sales and marketing people to show you smoke and mirrors, while getting ready to charge you for à la carte services that add up quickly. While the larger RPOs allow for perception of flexibility, the promise of Subject Matter Experts, and fast results, *they cannot do it faster, cheaper or better than you can internally.*

Once the honeymoon phase of onboarding a large global RPO firm is over, I've seen the allure quickly die off. There is not a lot of difference between the mechanics of what you can do internally and what an RPO does. The difference is 'how' it's done; most large RPO firms make no investment in the individuals working for them, and therefore, their employees are not invested in your company's success.

There are a few models for using RPOs. Let me share a sample of the most common ways they are used before we get into their application in companies like the ones you are leading at.

1. **All–In Model.** This is the end-to-end option and what an RPO firm is hoping you will choose. Think about it as an organization without a team of HR professionals doing sourcing, candidate development, assessment, scheduling, branding, etc. The RPO is literally doing all Talent Acquisition functions, and meeting with Hiring Managers as an internal Recruiter would. To the outside world, the RPO is part of your company because this is how they represent themselves in this model.

   Employees of the RPO might use a different email system and be located across the country, or they could sit in the same building as your CEO and use your email addresses. This type of contract is generally longer term – 1-3 years – and will involve significant start-up fees. The model is often complicated and inconsistent through negotiation. The fees could be monthly, pay-per-resource, or flat. RPO teams do a lot of discovery during the sales process, and part of this is looking for a strategy to maximize their profits at your organization. Your CFO and CHRO are often attracted to a cost-per-hire model, and this is because they don't see the additional costs that are attached. This is especially true for high volume hiring, because basic costs are seen on a flat, per month basis. It becomes very expensive, very quickly, when you have a high level job, or one-off that is charged at a pay-per-requisition open and close fee.

2. **Partial Model.** This is a specialized model that gives an RPO one or two pieces of your business. The parts you hand over are not at the core of your Talent Acquisition activity, and you'd keep that core 'mojo' work internal. It might be that the RPO only does the sourcing, or the back-end administrative work, like scheduling. They might take on your branding, offer letter processing, or candidate travel. These combinations can be arranged as their own packages, and the timelines of the contract are more flexible, allowing you to turn these services on and off quickly and as needed. This can be a very strategic way to manage your resources and get the best return on your investment.

3. **Contingent Model.** This option is often referred to as staff augmentation, or flux business. It's intended for short projects, and looks like compressed versions of The All-In or Partial. For example, I've seen a team of 65 internal Recruiters quadruple their workload in times of heavy hiring. For scenarios like these, it makes sense to implement an RPO. A company using this strategy might use the RPO for different markets. They may not have additional headcount dollars and need

temporary staff. It's a good option for virtual models where the RPO resources can be managed by a different company all together. You could opt for a charge-per-resource, per month in this model, and can outsource talent in the roles of Recruiter, Project Manager, or Recruiting Coordinator for a flat cost. Could you hire someone internally for less money? Yes. But that might not suit your needs for the short term.

These are the most common models you'll see, and many RPO firms sell you on the idea that they have a system, methodology, and process to optimize your Talent Acquisition function. In reality, they may not have *any* of that. It might just be their impressive sales function, and their ability to hire the same Recruiter that you might, but pay them less and charge you the mark-up. Without a proven model to make the RPO faster, cheaper and better, there is really no value with the All–In model.

If this is the case, how did the concept of using end-to-end RPOs capture so many people? Despite winning the hearts and minds of a variety of executives, many large global RPO firms haven't actually produced any of the results they initially promised.

WHY LARGE RPO ARRANGEMENTS ARE PROBLEMATIC

When RPO became popular around the millennium, the first large firms promised a sophisticated process they could use for many employers, and everyone would reap the benefits of scale. It didn't work. Not surprisingly, nobody wanted to mingle their recruiting with another employer. With the likelihood a conflict of interest in one firm using the same candidate pool for competitors, the economies of scale could not be achieved.

Large RPO firms often promise strategic talent dedicated to your business. They might have an excellent Project Manager (PM) on your account, but don't be fooled! That PM is working on nine other companies as well, and you (and all nine other clients) are paying 100% of this resource's time. You can likely find the same quality of hire for yourself and have all of their time dedicated to your business goals.

Many large RPO firms promise quality hires at a reasonable cost. What they actually deliver are scenarios like: if they fill a role with an internal hire, you will still pay for the hire as if they had been sourced from the start. They will also get a big fee if they hire an employee referral. You have to pay for each hire the same, even if a fantastic candidate fell into their lap. That's not what most people consider a reasonable cost. In some cases, RPO firms work, and work well. They can truly deliver in some cases, but don't be romanticized into thinking this is the rule – it is the exception, especially in the All–In models.

When you look at this model historically, it has not worked well for end-to-end Talent Acquisition needs. There have been issues with the delivery of getting to know your business, and helping you to scale quickly. A client of mine had a long history with RPOs before I worked with them. They had three internal Recruiters who were providing full cycle recruiting. This company decided to implement an RPO for non-core activities that were very time consuming. Sourcing was performed by the RPO as it kept the relationships intact between the Hiring Managers and the internal Recruiters. The gap they experienced was that after the internal Recruiter completed a fantastic intake meeting with the Hiring Manager and took the time to understand their business needs and the kind of talent they needed for the future, the sourcing team was not always getting this information. They were also not investing the time for knowledge exchange because employees of the RPO firm had many client groups to service. Now the first step in finding top talent was diluted without this exchange of key information. With a shared service model in many RPOs, the back engine of their team was changing weekly, so the clients weren't getting a consistent support team. This decreased the quality of candidates being sourced, and the Hiring Managers saw this immediately. The whole set up drowned quickly, so the RPO had to hire more Sourcers to keep a dedicated team on this client's work, which of course increased the cost to the client.

Another client of mine was a global company which had gone with the All–In model and outsourced its entire Talent Acquisition function. When speaking to the RPO-managed Recruiters – some who sat in the client's offices, and some who only worked from home – I asked how they liked working on behalf of the company. One of them told me that they hadn't been with the RPO long, and found the role through an ad in the local paper for a Recruiter position. It was listed as a role at the client's company, so they applied. To their surprise, it was actually the RPO firm they were interviewing to work for, and there was no infrastructure in place until they had a new client contract signed. The RPO firms scale their own business based on contracts – they hire Recruiters like you would inside a company. Then they tell the Recruiters that they work for the client, essentially making the RPO a *broker* of contingent labor. They are not a highly functioning machine using a proven system and methodology. Most of the time, when you hire the larger RPO firms, they hire other people to work on your behalf at that moment and ship them to another client, or let them go once your contract is over. Their employees get paid less, your company invests in their training on your systems and processes, and then you get to pay their employer a lot more money for this privilege.

Money talks. When hiring an RPO firm, there will be a lot of talk of cost for service. The issue is that many large RPO firms are notorious for not being transparent—or consistent—with their pricing. Unfortunately, these RPO firms don't want you to understand the cost of each line item they are charging you for, so it takes a lot to uncover how much you are actually paying for each service, and what your upfront payment covers. Many get stuck in a cycle of ongoing payments and complicated models that take you ages to break apart and bring in-house. When an RPO firm promises full cycle recruiting services, it takes a genius in Procurement along with HR to figure out what it actually costs. Think about it like the purchase of your enterprise software. It's important to understand the cost over the contract period, so if your contract is for three years, you need to know the costs all in. It needs to be done in a sophisticated way so you can compare the proposed products or services to internal resource costs. RPO firms can lead with cost-per-hire – but then you need to include the costs for all hires, even if they didn't source them, or you hired internally. You need to consider fees for opening and closing requisitions and all the other ways RPO firms have decided to raise the cost to your business.

I've seen many occasions where the HR leader ends up hating their full scale RPO model because they want more sourcing and branding, or social media support. However, when they inquire about these services, it turns out that the package they have doesn't include anything but the cost-per-hire. Everything is extra, and *it is not cheap*. Remember, many large RPO firms are only the *broker* of services; they make money per service, and they are good at it.

AN AREA WHERE RPO IS VERY VALUABLE

As I opened the chapter with, there is a time and place to use RPO and get a good return on your investment. It's not just in Europe, where using an RPO is a normal cultural practice for large global companies. The contingent option I outlined earlier is key in this. Especially if you look at smaller companies without a budget to hire a full Talent Acquisition organization. You will be able to scale more quickly by using an RPO strategy, and this is where you can get a lot of value. If you only have one HR person, and they oversee 50-100 employees, and your CEO is looking for a 100% growth rate in the next 12 months, this is the moment. This is where considering using RPO as a resource can help you be successful. It's important to remember that it's a moment in time and only a portion of the business.

If you have a sudden need for growth that isn't forecasted, or have a sudden need to create a new hub, say 200 hires in 4 months, then we recommend using an RPO model from a small or mid-sized firm. This can offer your team more augmentation and scalability – and they are more specialized for the needs of smaller organizations.

Another effective use of an RPO is for diverse and far-stretched geographic or specific expertise requirements. A Talent Acquisition function needs to be really good at sourcing and finding the core key job areas within their company. Outside of that, you are likely adding more value to your company by Project Managing purchased services than doing that non-core work yourself. In addition, many RPO companies are unbundling their services in unique ways. You might find that for the one or two things you want to take outside of your team, this is an area to invest some time learning about.

RPO AND ASSOCIATED COSTS

Wall Street does not like headcount. It's true, and it sometimes means that spending more money to avoid headcount costs is seen as the better decision. This notion can make RPO firms very crafty about how they approach you, and how you get tangled into their web. Like any large contract, once you're in, it's difficult to extricate yourself.

In a large services company headquartered in the US, their head of Talent Acquisition was managing a high volume operation for the global team – much of it done through RPO. There were many different roles to fill, and they had a need for continuity of experience. When they had a change in Talent Acquisition leadership, the new leader's first order of business was to re-evaluate the return on investment on the RPO. The leader took a lot of flak for starting this process as the company was so used to running through RPO, and were very change averse.

To bring the function back in-house, the leader had to show what service levels could be, what costs could be, and how a transition would help the business without a negative impact. They went through many rounds of expectation setting, even having to challenge their CHRO, who was against bringing it in-house – mostly due to headcount costs. This Talent Acquisition leader had to build trust and really understand the business concerns in the current model. The quality of hires was low, the costs were high, and yet there was still a fear of change.

An in-house Talent Acquisition function was the business-minded return on investment approach though. It proved that region by region, and business group by business group, that the company was not getting value for their money. In this instance, all the investment of time on the front-end has paid dividends over and over. It took courage and a lot of hard work. The selling points that really helped the leaders at this company change were understanding the business needs, and then showing a financial comparison side-by-side on the costs. With this analysis, it was easy to see that the business was paying for a Cadillac, and driving a beat-up Chevy. Once they got their heads around these facts, it was no longer a hard sell. To complete the story, the internal Talent Acquisition was faster, better, cheaper, more engaged, and provided better quality hires. And, while attempting to do so this quickly is not recommended, this team completed the separation from the RPO over a three week transition period, completing it in five business days on the US side, and within a few months in Europe. Leaders at the services company *LOVE* the internal Talent Acquisition team and what they bring to the table; quality hires, more invested employees, and more value to the business.

In the end, the cost versus the value for full RPO models doesn't pan out. These brokers of contingent staff sell you on the end-to-end recruiting experience. In reality, they sign a contract, they hire people, post jobs online, and then pay those staff only 60-70% of what they charge you. That Recruiter has no experience with your brand, no relationships with your Hiring Managers, and can offer nothing more than your internal team can. When you offload this labor, you're getting contingent staff without any process expertise, without that 'mojo' that makes your internal team so effective. It's the bag of potato chips you were so craving, and when you opened the large bag, there was only one chip. It was a good chip, but not nearly enough to satisfy you, and definitely fell short of what you thought you paid for.

In lean economic times, it's vital that companies ensure they keep people who are passionate and are great at their job, even if they need to reduce their recruiting function. An investment in training and development for people is also critical. As Talent Acquisition teams focus on demonstrating their value, and then delivering on that promise, the leader of the function needs to reinforce how important this is. Even when the company is not growing at 100%. In one of the most competitive job economies we've ever seen, organizations have a very difficult time in trying to recruit and attract the people they want. It really is a war for talent at times and good people are harder to extricate out of their current job to come work for an organization. Your business needs real people who are passionate about your organization to build relationships and sell your Employer Brand.

And it's not always only about hiring people. I see a lot of organizations asking for things like optimizing the recruiting and staffing functions, and making their HR teams more effective. Consultants are doing a lot more training and development of Recruiters and HR employees. There is also more investment in university and recruiting programs. These investments are not made in vain, and once these areas are operating at their full potential, then and only then, can you enter the RPO space to see what functions, if any, to outsource. A good consultant can help with these decisions and help you make a smoother transition by brokering the relationship between the RPO firm and your organization.

REVIEWING YOUR EXISTING RPO

The right firm's role is to help an internal staffing function that is managing the core responsibility of recruiting. The flexibility they can give your organization to scale quickly and to manage time-consuming processes that your team is not skilled at, is very valuable. They can also perform the functions that you do not manage internally, or candidate relationships, very effectively. You are the Talent Acquisition lead because you know your business. You inspire your internal talent to want to succeed by having incredible relationships with Hiring Managers, candidates, and their HR partners.

Don't give all that away to get the headcount off your payroll – as you can see, it will cost you more than you realize!

Review your RPO agreement and see what you are actually getting for the money you are spending. Compare it to what it would cost you to run Talent Acquisition internally. You don't need any fancy math at this point, the return on investment you bring is very clear when you look at the numbers, and no successful business wants to throw away hard earned dollars.

Think about your quality of hire. It's not just a trendy metric – it can be the difference between your team winning, or losing. How do you know you're hiring top talent? Well, they help your company earn money by bringing skills that are needed today, and tomorrow. You know what these skills are because you are part of the organization and you live and breathe its success. Many large global RPO firms live and breathe *their own* profits which are far away from your business objectives. Their goal is to fill open requisitions so they can charge you when you close them. Filling the job is very different than finding the right talent that your business needs. RPO employees lack the bridge of knowledge and passion to think about what your business needs in the future. They may not be filling your organization with the best talent; only with available talent.

I advocate, and loudly, to keep recruiting for core jobs internal. You should want to own this part of your business because *you can do it better, faster and cheaper*, if it's done right. Sure, take the non-core job responsibility and outsource them if the conditions are right for your business. But know that nobody will understand the needs of those core functions better than you and your team.

CONCLUSION

Working to build and grow relationships internally and externally takes a lot of time and effort – but it pays off in spades. Prioritization is key, and asking for help is a good thing. If your non-core jobs can be easily outsourced and turned on and off with the use of a small or mid-sized RPO, then go for it! The All-In model has you handing off your greatest opportunity to bring value to your team! It may also bring the overall quality down and drive costs up which does not make good business sense.

Some organizations are figuring out the misperception that a full RPO saves money. In the long run, as businesses continue to dig deep, they can see that RPOs actually cost more money. Don't be late to the party in learning what your organization is actually getting for the money you might be spending. Continue to be the strategic partner and trusted advisor that Talent Acquisition needs, and say "No thank you." You can read a longer article I've published on this topic at RecruitCONSULT.net

Next, we'll turn our attention inward to the topic that many Talent Acquisition professionals either love or dread: organizational politics.

CHAPTER 8: ORGANIZATIONAL POLITICS

Identifying and recruiting the best possible people for your organization is a challenging task. But the biggest battles you may face as a leader may be internal. The reality of the role of a corporate Talent Acquisition leader is that often the most difficult part of the job is navigating organizational politics.

You've probably been in one of these situations before:

- Other HR team members block you from access to key Hiring Managers or other key people. Others seem to undermine your success.

- You have to get someone else in the organization (Corporate Communications, Purchasing, and Legal) to do something so you can accomplish a task, but they are not helping or doing what you know you need.

- You have Hiring Managers who are not respectful of the Talent Acquisition function and who are constantly second guessing you—or worse, speaking poorly about you to others in the organization.

- Your boss is constantly riding you about your performance, yet you feel trapped because you do not feel in control of the outcome of your team's work (because your Hiring Managers are dragging their feet or for other reasons).

- Search firms and other third-party agencies try to run around you and go directly to your Hiring Managers, making you feel as though you're a fifth wheel.

There are so many more situations like this that may involve all of the various constituencies we touch:

- Hiring Managers

- Candidates

- Members of the interview team

- HR Generalists

- Third-party Recruiting (TPR) professionals

- Administrative and coordinating staff

- Your boss

Your job as a Talent Acquisition professional is one of the most politically charged roles in business. Politics are a fact of life, and we must recognize that any time two or more people work together or hang out at the watercooler together, there will always be politics.

Here are some common manifestations of office politics:

- Manipulation of peers

- "I'll scratch your back if you scratch mine"

- Looking out for #1

- Destructiveness

- Covert under-the-table deals

- Backstabbing

- One-upmanship

- Deceitfulness

- Turf battles

- Petty personal squabbles

- Looking good without substance

- Back-room decisions

- Power plays and getting rid of rivals

- Behind-the-scenes maneuvering

- Brown-nosing

- Hidden agendas

When most people are asked if they want to engage in organizational politics, they typically insist that they do not. But when people are asked if they want to get better at being more *politically savvy,* they say, "Yes!"

Professional Talent Acquisition teams must embrace the skill of being politically savvy. The fact is that for the savvy Recruiter the arena of office politics presents opportunities to leverage your political muscle.

Informal Influence

As leaders we must recognize that informal influence shapes the organization. Because of this we must recognize that how we interact with different people inside the organization may be different than the way we interact with others. We must be able to alter our delivery and interaction style with different types of people.

Different values combine with different levels of activeness to produce a diversity of political styles. It's easy to see how people's values about organizational politics are likely to shape the political style they adopt. The more negatively managers view politics, the less likely they are to engage in it. The reverse is not true. It turns out that the activeness of a person is not a good predictor of how he or she values organizational politics.

THE POLITICAL STYLE GRID

Using the three value and three action orientations, you can place yourself—or a colleague—on the Political Style Grid. The horizontal dimension designates the value orientation and moves from "negative" to "neutral" to "positive." The vertical dimension indicates the action orientation in increasing order from "responds" to "predicts" to "initiates."

Politics viewed as:

		Negative	Neutral	Positive
		Machiavellian	**Responsible**	**Leader**
Action Orientation	**Initiates**	- Manipulator - Looks out for #1	- Obligation - Comes with Territory	- Play Maker - Impact Player
		Protector	**Speculator**	**Advisor**
	Predicts	- File Builder - Defensive	- Grapeviner	- Counselor
		Cynic	**Fatalist**	**Spectator**
	Responds	- I told you so - Gossip	- Que Sera Sera	- Fan - Encourager

Source: Joel DeLuca, PhD, *Political Savvy, Systematic Approaches to Leadership Behind the Scenes*

Politics are a fact of organizational life. If you can get past the political blind spot by breaking through the moral and rational blocks then you can choose to move into the active portion of the Political Style Grid.

The Interest Grid

Politically active managers can use organizational politics for good or bad. Any working definition of organizational politics should contain these possibilities. Politics in organizations are typically boiled down to self-interest and how it plays out in the organization.

Interest Grid

Source: Joel DeLuca, PhD, *Political Savvy, Systematic Approaches to Leadership Behind the Scenes*

The upper left-hand corner, **dysfunctional politics**, is where the nasty "Machiavellian" leaders live. Like the subject of Machiavelli's 1532 classic *The Prince*, the "Mach" is only interested in advancing his or her personal ambitions, while going to great lengths to appear to benefit the organization. Dysfunctional politics occur when individuals promote their own interests at the expense of the organization. An example is a manager who agrees with the boss' idea while knowing it's not a good idea. Approval by a superior is gained at the eventual expense of the organization.

The upper right corner, **functional politics**, signifies actions primarily aimed at benefiting the organization. This area is where the politically savvy dwell. It represents the ideal of the organization system and the goal of effective organization design. Organizations are set up under the principle that the best way to achieve one's own interests is to benefit the whole. Dysfunctional politics is based upon self-interest. While functional politics is motivated by enlightened self-interest, the savvy operate chiefly in the functional politics zone. Being savvy doesn't mean being dumb about one's own career. It does mean putting the organization's interests first.

While the active players generally stay in the upper two quadrants, there are times when they can end up in the bottom two. When conflicts arise between organization and personal interests, savvy players may take the "sacrificial hit," giving up some of their own personal agenda for the good of the organization. While it may sound noble—and sometimes it actually is—it can also be smart.

Since the orientation of the savvy Recruiter is to do what they think is right for the organization, it is natural for them to put the interests of the organization first.

They also know that a reputation for putting aside personal agendas builds credibility. However, few savvy individuals spend a great deal of time operating in this area. If they do, they eventually burn out or develop martyr syndromes. Now, the Machs love martyrs. A skillful appeal to the martyrs' nobility can turn them into kamikazes for the Machs' own personal agendas.

Very few people last long in the bottom left corner.

Managing Office Paranoia

Here's the deal: on-the-job paranoia is part of the world of corporate politics, so you need to learn to work it. In fact, Andy Grove, former head of Intel, is famous for the slogan, *"Only the paranoid survive."* He was stating that publicly in terms of his competition, but frankly it applies internally too.

What's going on in today's corporate environment that can fuel your paranoia? Plenty. Bad people can stab you in the back. Really bad people can stab you in the front. Internal competitors won't bother moving your cheese—they'll just steal it.

There are whisper campaigns and watercooler gossip sessions. Rivals will take credit for your successes and dump failures at your door. They'll shamelessly tell your boss that you aren't pulling your weight and then head out to the golf course for an afternoon of "networking" while you work on a shared project.

You could be cut out of the loop. Behind your back you could be categorized as either a pain in the neck or as nonessential.

In short, anything that happens in "Dilbert" ("Dilbert" the satirical office humor comic strip by Scott Adams) can happen to you.

Symptoms of Paranoia and How to Cure Them

The only way to not have fear of sharks is to be a bigger shark. Become the leader of the sharks. Let your peers know that if they mess with you, they will regret it.

As a consultative Talent Acquisition group leader, you must openly reward good, ethical, non-creepy behavior, and you must come down hard on would-be office Machiavellians. Here are some common pitfalls and how you and your team can overcome them.

- **Hoarding Information.** Paranoid people believe that keeping information to themselves gives them an advantage. This backfires when co-workers stop sharing their good ideas. You and your team members need to think strategically. Who's best qualified to solve problems? Who can help the team exploit what they know to mutual advantage?

- **Mistrusting Subordinates.** If you're involved with every detail because you're afraid your direct reports or co-workers will mess it up, you have a problem. Get over it! Entrust your people with something you don't care about and then build from there. Your newly empowered employees are likely to do a better job than you would have.

- **The "Cc" Line is Never Empty.** Paranoid employees want to make sure everyone knows when they have a good idea. So, they copy the whole company on e-mails. Don't do this. Mass e-mails generate mass annoyance, especially when they're designed to stroke one's ego. E-mail only the appropriate people, and focus on how your accomplishment helps them.

- **Lunching Alone.** Isolation is a not a good means of protection. The higher you rise, the more big-shots have to sign off on your next move. Who you don't know will hold you back. Work creates a one-dimensional perception of others. If you get to know your colleagues outside of the cube-farm, you'll realize they're not all plotting against you—and if they know you as a human being they'll be less likely to stab you in the back.

TRIANGULATION

When discussing a sensitive or volatile issue, we really don't use the word "no." We can express ourselves professionally using different words. Triangulate your conversations by talking about the issue or problem and not making the conversation about the other party.

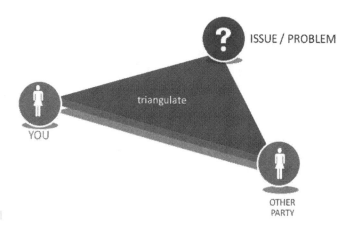

Remove the word "you" from your conversation—take out the personalization. When you push back, be prepared to back up your statements with facts from your knowledge or research. If you are very passionate about an issue, take time to formulate your argument and then go back.

Going over the heads of others almost always complicates issues. Don't be tempted to go to someone's boss to get someone to do something or to complain. In almost every case, situations can be improved by talking directly to the individual. Here are some tips for working with different groups:

HR Generalists are our partners. We need to first learn how we can partner with them effectively. First of all, remember we and HR Generalists are validated by our "likeability" and "credibility" factors by our Hiring Managers and business leaders. The moment we recognize that we both want the same credibility with our Hiring Managers we can work together. There is no winner in this contest. More about this later!

Others inside the organization (Legal, Purchasing, Communications) are often viewed by us as "blockers." We must recognize that they have a job to do, and their view is that their job is often more important than yours. Instead of viewing their role as blockers, get to know these people and engage them before there is a need. Share with them your ultimate goal of the project and ask them how "we" can achieve the goal. Using words like "I need you to do X" are not productive. Enlist these teams as partners for you.

When dealing with **third-party search professionals** (TPRs), contracting is the key to success. Manage expectations and clarify who, what, and when things need to get done. And get over it. Third-party Recruiters are not our enemy. They are a valuable tool in our toolbox. Understand that if you and the TPR work together as a team, the business wins.

With **Hiring Managers**, always manage expectations and always follow up. Never assume that they understand anything about your process. Always clarify what you understand their needs are, what you are going to do, what they are going to do, and what others are going to do in the process. Never avoid confrontation with Hiring Managers; always follow up and communicate even if there is nothing good to share. No news is bad news. Always tout your successes, but do it effectively by asking your happy clients to share the good news. If there are problems, deal with them now.

MANAGING YOUR TALENT ACQUISITION TEAM'S INTERNAL BRAND

It's all about relationships, and part of the relationship is based on perception. How you and your team are perceived, and the watercooler chat about the department, is vital to success (or in some unfortunate cases, killers of success). This is often referred to as *internal branding*. It is essentially what others are saying about you and if it's already good, protect it because a lot can depend on this.

It's not likely you will have a Public Relations team ready to step in and help you if you're in need of reputation management, but there are many things you can do to create and positively position your team's internal brand. If you approach this as a Publicist approaches a celebrity you will often start with the "differentiator" or what makes your team different than other methods the organization could use for Talent Acquisition. What are your successes, and what are the things you can admit to improving on? Actors, when being recognized at the Oscars, are generally humble and recognize everyone involved in their success. Make sure you collect any good press about individual performance and the team as well; having business leaders sing your praises and act as advocates helps spread the word of the value Talent Acquisition adds.

Another Public Relations tip that works well is preparation of your spokespeople. Teaching your Recruiters to be confident with all audiences, respond to rumors, and answer questions professionally (and with specific responses) is critical to the internal brand. This will impact credibility, act as a driver for change management when working with the Hiring Managers, and keep the invitations to planning meetings coming. Interacting well with others will impact your ability to help the business set realistic goals and will change the position of *having* to work with you to *wanting* to work with you.

Without clear goals and expectations, it will be hard to establish your desired internal brand. The goals you want your organization to know about are the ones that will benefit everyone in the long run. Consider naming your initiatives and make each goal its own project to be managed; this will also create Leadership opportunities within your team, keeping the team motivated. As you achieve your goals (not your plan), take advantage of the new spokespeople on your team from the dialogue training.

The last lesson taken from Public Relations is the basics of crisis communication. How you address problems and problem areas will greatly influence the perception of the team. Whether it's a rogue rumor, unsuccessful Hiring Manager, or a performance issue on the team, *do not* hide from it. "No comment" will not help your reputation. Address the issues right away with transparency and immediacy.

TAKING THINGS ONE STEP FURTHER

Part of creating a strong internal brand is about accomplishments, but sharing your checked off to-do list isn't enough. To take things one step further, consider positioning the great work that is in progress and accomplished against business objectives, for example:

- If the business wants to grow by 30% in 2 quarters, show how you are going to achieve this or make a more realistic recommendation up front to help guide sound business decisions.

- Produce progress reports that show forecasted growth beside what you are actually recruiting; highlight productivity.

- Share the new relationships your sourcing team has established with professional associations and emerging programs at the university level in preparation for hard-to-find skills or skills that have drastically changed in the market in recent years.

It's one thing to say you're meeting your own goals but a whole other to achieve the things your business cares about. When you look at your accomplishments, before posting, ask yourself, "If I were a Hiring Manager, would I care about what is being shared?" Take your accomplishments one step further so that your internal partners can sit back and say, "Yes, I need that team at the table. They understand what I want and deliver!"

Plugging at the Right Place and Time

There are so many ways you can plug the team, the services, and your own value-add. Finding the right opportunities and times will make the difference in perception between sharing accomplishments and showboating. Some opportunities you may want to take advantage of are already in place; it's just a matter of adding content and context.

In Person
- Regularly scheduled business meetings are an ideal place to add Talent Acquisition updates and highlight positive metrics. Being prepared and well-spoken in front of your department and executives is important for aligning goals and understanding challenges. Your agenda should

include hires versus plans, Talent Acquisition priorities, strategies, training, flow of the business (including general recruiting events), and candidate feedback.

- Quarterly "town hall" events for business leaders allow for a bigger picture focus. This can include providing updates on strategies and programs as well as their ROI. Feedback from candidates regarding Hiring Managers is always better delivered in person and should be reviewed regularly.

Virtually
- Your existing intranet is a powerful tool and is perfect for measuring the interest of the information you are sharing. Selecting the appropriate hiring metrics and high-profile projects (that you have named) to share with specific audiences helps to form your internal brand. Dividing by Hiring Manager or department may be welcome at some organizations as well (not to create competition, so be cognizant of what you post and who is able to see it).

- A weekly communiqué (e-mail, blog) to the business and Talent Acquisition/ HR teams providing an overview of progress, process, events, and requests for feedback are often well received and can be easily filed for later reading.

- Enterprise social tools (Yammer, Jive, Slack, etc.) to foster two-way dialogue and breakdown geographic boundaries. They also allow the conversation threads to live on for anyone who may be looking for an update later on.

As much as we as human beings would like to believe that any human, given the appropriate opportunity and context, can get along with any other human, in the corporate environment it's sometimes just not going to happen. Like the dog and the cat who live in the same household, despite an outward appearance of harmony (especially when food is provided), occasional flare-ups are inevitable. In our case, the cats and dogs are Talent Acquisition specialists and HR Generalists.

THE TRUE GRIT BETWEEN HR GENERALISTS AND RECRUITERS

One day I was sitting at my desk as head of Talent Acquisition for one of the large companies I used to work for when I received a frantic call from the head of HR of one of our divisions complaining about some recruiting we were doing for one of her managers.

"The manager's not happy with you," she growled. "You know the turnover rate for Financial Planners and Analysts is high. The only way we can keep those jobs filled is to keep the pipeline packed with candidates, and the manager's hardly seen any candidates!"

"Why's that?" I replied. "We're doing the work sending you candidates." "Yeah, but the quality's low."

"Says who?" I asked.

"Us. HR. Our job is to make sure the Hiring Managers taken care of."

"Okay, so we're sending you candidates but they're not getting past HR?"

"Exactly. And now the Hiring Manager's all over my back for results." "So why don't we send the candidates to the Hiring Manager first?" I said.

"Because, Jeremy, *we* have to screen them first—that's our job."

"No, your job is to make sure the Hiring Manager's taken care of—you said so yourself—and in this case, taking care of the Hiring Manager means they need to see a volume of candidates to be reassured the pipeline is filled. Why don't we try an experiment? Let's send the candidates to the Hiring Manager to assess technical fit, then to you to assess the cultural fit, then see where we stand."

I can't tell you how often I've seen a version of the above scenario played out in companies. Without a doubt, during the last few years the relationship between HR Generalists and in-house Recruiters has become more complex. In an economic downturn many Generalists may be asked to do more recruiting because resources are limited. When the economy rebounds it's tempting to think the roles will revert back to normal. But will they? And if so, how have things changed or stayed the same? Have we learned anything at all through the last few economic rollercoasters about how we can work more effectively together, or have we moved further apart?

Part of the problem is endemic to these two jobs and rooted in the fabric and fundamental DNA of these roles as they have evolved over time. But fortunately, as human beings (and not simply as organisms in nature), by identifying these built-in barriers to success, we can adapt, formulate a way around the barriers, and beat evolution! (Or at least understand how to succeed and survive).

To begin, it would be helpful to provide some information on the historical challenges, or "True Grit," in the relationship between Recruiters and Generalists from each of their perspectives and also on what has worked in the past. So, let's hear from both sides. Here's a story from the point of view of the HR Generalist.

The Recruiter and the Generalist

Without first discussing with the Generalist, the company Hiring Manager told the Recruiter that he had a position that he wanted filled. Driven for results and action-oriented, the Recruiter developed the job profile, went to the compensation manager, got the suggested pay range, started sourcing candidates, and selected the interviewing panel with the Hiring Manager.

The Generalist found out through secondhand information. She contacted the Recruiter and told him to present all candidates for her to screen *before* the Hiring Manager.

The Recruiter verbally agreed but sourced candidates and sent them directly to the Hiring Manager for the Hiring Manager's feedback. The Hiring Manager's Administrative Assistant scheduled the interviews from which the Generalist was accidentally omitted. When the successful candidate was selected, the Recruiter extended the verbal offer.

Thereafter the Recruiter followed protocol and reached out to the Generalist to have her draft and send the written offer, but the situation was challenging because the Recruiter didn't recognize the value that the Generalist brought to the relationship. The Generalist may have been able to share information about the role, the Hiring Manager, or culture of the group that could have been helpful to the Recruiter, possibly even resulting in a quicker hire. The Generalist also had information about other roles and salaries within the organization and could have provided valuable guidance to the Recruiter on the offer, like helping to maintain internal equity. Overall, the Recruiter could have leveraged the Generalist to support the process from helping to develop the hiring strategy to on-boarding.

These experiences are symptomatic of the challenges in the relationship between these two functions. Here's one problem: the role of HR Generalist touches on many important areas of a company—organizational development and change, employee relations, compensation and benefits, and conflict resolution. But as a partner to general managers running a business, a lot of what an HR Generalist deals with tends to be "negative" in nature (for instance, when there's an employee conflict or problem, who does the manager call? The HR Generalist). Success for the HR Generalist can often be helping a company *avoid disaster*.

By contrast, a Recruiter's success is usually "positive" in nature. Success for them is not preventing failure but *adding* to a company in the form of identifying, sourcing, and assessing a new hire. Since more often than not Talent Acquisition is one of the many responsibilities that fall under the purview of HR, when a recruiting opportunity arises, it's only natural that the HR Generalist will want to get involved and participate in a process where a successful result is a refreshing "positive" for his or her portfolio. Many times, there is a stylistically differing approach to solving problems—Recruiters see a lot of black and white, while Generalists see a lot of grey.

Here are some other built-in problems:

Role Clarity. Often there is a lack of understanding of what each side brings to the table in terms of how they support the recruiting process from strategy to offer preparation and extension. The result is frequently a less than optimal relationship versus the complimentary partnership that it can and should be.

Focus. A Recruiter's main focus is all about getting the job done and anything that impedes that, including an intrusive HR Generalist, must be overcome (in fact, third-party, outside recruiting companies often train their professionals in strategies for how to circumvent HR professionals).

Contact. An HR executive relies on a lot of face-to-face contact with a Hiring Manager to build trust and rapport. More often than not, this helps them become a line manager's go-to person. Similarly, more often than not (and I would argue most of the time), in order for Recruiters to be successful, they need to have direct access to the Hiring Manager. This can be perceived as getting into HR's space, which is why HR Generalists frequently want to see themselves as the client. Generalists often feel like they have better or closer relationships with a client and therefore can speak on the client's behalf. At times Generalists think they know even better than the client and may impede direct lines of communication between the Recruiter and client. But if the Recruiter is blocked from seeing the Hiring Manager, the search will often fail.

Metrics. Recruiters often measure their own success and self-worth in a company by taking a look around and identifying all the faces they were responsible for bringing into the organization. Recruiters view their own success by the impact they've made on the company in this way and, as such, want to be recognized and given credit for this.

However, there's something going on here that isn't being mentioned: the competition to prove who is adding the most value to the company between the HR Generalist and Talent Acquisition professional. But here's the biggest problem, the one that trumps all others: *the Hiring Manager doesn't care.* They just want the jobs filled and the work done, preferably with as little interruption to them as possible.

Thus, in order to improve the situation, the most important thing is for Recruiter and HR Generalist to recognize that their mutual survival depends on the success of this process and that they each bring unique skills and expertise to contribute to its success. *Respect and trust are key.* Even though they may not totally understand where their partners are coming from, each has to give the other the benefit of the doubt and seek to understand their role and the context in which they operate. Developing an understanding and appreciation for what each other does and the different skill sets that are required to perform each role is essential. A Generalist and a Recruiter have very different jobs, and each have distinct areas of specialty. It takes respect for what each other does to serve as the foundation for a good partnership.

The Recruiter needs to recognize the HR Generalist's value. They can be great at understanding the business and the culture, provide insight into management, and most importantly, they understand the unspoken subtle motivations and drivers of an organization, without which no one, including the best candidate, can succeed. Conversely, the HR Generalist needs to acknowledge that the Recruiter is gifted at building bridges between the company and candidates on the outside, attracting quality people, assessing them, stewarding them through the process, and "closing" candidates. Here are steps both parties can take:

- **Respect**. Both parties acknowledge that they need to be perceived as adding value in the Talent Acquisition process.

- **Communication.** Keeping partners informed builds trust and understanding. You need to keep your partners in the know. Good communication skills are important. Commencing when a Hiring Manager identifies a hiring need, the Generalist should communicate with the Recruiter the need that has been identified so the two can work together throughout the hiring process.

- **Agreement.** A small SLA can be worked out between Recruiter and HR that would outline the goals and responsibilities of each and how they work together. The SLA can be written or verbal, depending on the culture, and can address the following issues:

  o *Communication between HR Generalist and Recruiter during the Recruiting process.* How involved does the HR Generalist want to be in the assignment(s)? Do they want to be kept in the loop? If so, how often? In what form (e-mail, phone calls)? What would be the content?

○ *Communication between the Hiring Manager (the client) and HR Generalist/Recruiter.* How will the HR Generalist and Recruiter communicate the progress/status of the search to the Hiring Manager? Who will do it? Will it be jointly? Once this is clarified, many sticky and often times offending (to one party or the other) situations can be avoided such as one party trying to take credit for something in a meeting where all are present or another agreeing with the Hiring Manager to curry favor with the client.

○ The role of the HR Generalist in the interview process.

○ Who will make the offer to the successful candidate and "close the deal"?

○ Who will follow up and turn away unsuccessful candidates?

○ *Candidate follow-up.* Both parties have to recognize relationships have been made in this process with both successful and unsuccessful candidates.

○ *Relationship assessment.* Candidate and Hiring Manager satisfaction surveys can be sent to all constituents involved in the process as a mirror to how the relationship has worked (and the effectiveness of a service level agreement, if used). Formal surveys can accomplish this but what's most important is dialogue between all parties.

As we all know Talent Acquisition scenarios come in all shapes and sizes. There are times when situations dictate the Hiring Manager has one and only one point of contact and that has to be the HR Generalist; similarly, at other times that one point of contact is the Recruiter and the Recruiter only. Regardless of the situation, communication and trust between the Recruiter and HR Generalist will ultimately only benefit both.

So how do you build trust when the relationship is new, and neither party has much of a clue about the other? Spend time in people's offices, and make deposits in to the emotional bank account. Don't be defensive and try to explain issues away. Own the current state, work to create a shared solution, and stay positive. *Criticize in private and praise in public.*

If a problem arises, one of the parties may need to take the high road and initiate dialogue. Both parties need to own up to the current state of the relationship and the roles that each has played in creating the current state. They need to be willing to actively listen to the other party and address what isn't working and commit to making necessary changes in their *own* behavior.

That's where something written along the lines of a service level agreement can be very effective. At a minimum it will enable both parties to present a unified, team approach to the client, to the benefit of everyone involved. Once that's in place both parties can build a pattern of trust over time and safely witness and participate in the "paradox" that leads to ultimate success.

Remember that HR division head who called me irritated and in a panic because her client wasn't seeing enough candidates for a particular role (they weren't getting past HR)? She tried my suggestion that the client meet the candidates first to assess technical fit and HR second to assess cultural fit, and it worked! She realized that by taking a step back, by being involved in a different way and having less upfront "glory," paradoxically she could, and did, have greater success. We all did, and that's the whole point: when you boil it down, we all work for the same company, and we're all working toward consistently building HR's credibility in the company. In the end we all know that an HR department that's not credible is the death knell for a business.

So that's why I can't decide if the relationship between Recruiter and HR Generalist is like husband and wife or brother and sister. Either way, it's all in the same family, or as we know from Darwin, it's all about "the survival of the family."

CONCLUSION

If Charles Darwin were to come back to life and instead of studying tortoise shells on the Galápagos Islands he spent a few months hanging out at the watercooler at Ajax Global Corporation, he would no doubt return home more firmly convinced than ever of the truth of the survival of the fittest. Office politics can be brutal, and especially so for consultative Recruiters who must, from time to time, speak truth to power, even if a chorus of ninnies proclaims that the Recruiter is a dangerous anarchist.

But others have survived and even triumphed in the office, and so can you. Play hard, play fair, and watch your back. Reward those who support you and beware of those who are envious. And above all be a great coach to your team. There is no greater antidote to office poison than a winning record.

CHAPTER 9: THE POWER OF RELATIONSHIPS

In 1992, I got a job as a Recruiter responsible for hiring Sales Representatives. Business was booming, and I had more than enough candidates—and perhaps because of that, I was arrogant. I let many candidates whom I chose not to hire simply slip away without calling them or following up.

Not long after that I was at a job fair, and some of the candidates I had interviewed for the sales representative role approached me. In front of my relatively new colleagues, they pulled no punches and criticized me for not being professional and getting back to them.

As embarrassed as I was to hear it, my accusers were right! I had dropped the ball and not treated them professionally. What I had not realized (even though I had experienced the same thing during my own period of being laid off) was that during recessionary times everything we do as Recruiters gets magnified.

Times of economic difficulty put us under a microscope in which perceptions are skewed. However, so too do they present great opportunities to build even better relationships with people outside of our organization (candidates, vendors, and third-party search providers) to sharpen our recruiting skills and enable us to be unique professionals who stand out from the pack.

But to begin, let's be clear: it's an ugly world out there. Your company may have gone through layoffs and decimated its Talent Acquisition department. And now you're the one who's left—and you still have to fill requisitions and hire people.

On top of all that, for many roles you need to fill (such as in Sales, Operations, and General Management) it can be harder to attract passive recruits during difficult times than in good times.

Fast forward to today and there are a whole new set of challenges. Candidates are much more entrepreneurial and willing to try their hand at consulting, freelancing, or innovating as an independent. There are new 'carrots' to compete for the best talent and very different desires for overall compensation than even a few years ago. With all the generations in the workplace, it becomes much more difficult to create a one-size-fits-all total compensation package that meets the needs of new and top talent.

BUILDING RELATIONSHIPS WITH *ALL* CANDIDATES

Challenging economic times require a greater focus on candidate management. With so many people looking for work and resumes coming in at a fast rate, there are simply more candidates to manage. Thus, for Recruiters who are usually very good at this, it's easier to drop the ball, and for those who usually don't do so well to begin with, it's worse. And as mentioned above, people usually magnify their experience during difficult times, and any slip-up will be judged much more harshly during a downturn than when things are good.

But the converse is also true (which is why this is a great opportunity for relationship building): those with whom you followed up and treated well will never forget how you stood out from the rest of the pack of potential employers who never called them back.

And remember, since the way you act reflects how your company is perceived, the way you treat people during this time can define your employer brand.

Therefore, as a common courtesy, you should immediately send an e-mail to all candidates who submitted a resume for a role. This can be automated through an applicant tracking system.

However, for those who have come in for an interview but did not get an offer, it is vital you follow up with them personally. Sending an e-mail in this instance is not only bad form, it's cowardly. E-mails are a one-way form of communication that provide no interaction, can be passed on to others, and don't allow you to develop a broader relationship with candidates.

It's important for you to prioritize which of these candidates to contact first and then to set aside time to make the calls. I recommend blocking out time at the end of the day, at five o'clock. Because it's later in the day, you may have to leave a message. If you do, don't leave the reason you're calling on their voice mail (that's the same as sending an e-mail). Instead leave a message simply asking for them to call you back. Then, once you do get them on the phone, be straightforward and genuine.

To review, here are some reminders for candidate follow-through:

- Prioritize which candidates to call first.

- Set aside time to make the calls.

- Call—don't send a letter or e-mail.

- If you have to leave a message, don't say why you're calling.

- Once you talk to them, be straightforward and genuine.

- Network with them for the future (even ask for referrals).

- Don't worry about the legal issues of turning them down on the phone.

Talent Acquisition lives on the economic cycle and rides the wave which goes up and down. We all wish for high waves, but of course there are low times too. Generally, the Talent Acquisition function is at the leading edge of change of those waves. The long and short is that we have to look for the long haul and maintain brand and candidate experience on up and down cycles. Don't forget there *will* be cycles and they need to be managed properly. As the Talent Acquisition leader, you won't have every resource in low times, so be prepared for that. Be prepared and anticipate changes in economy and manage through the fact you'll go up and down.

Talent Acquisition during lean times also forces you to hone and sharpen your skills. For instance, with active candidates, economic downturns require more investigation skills and a greater focus on candidate evaluation. Remember our earlier discussion of considering all candidates – simply because someone is laid off doesn't mean they are a bad candidate. However, it does require greater investigation to ensure that there aren't performance issues.

And, as mentioned, passive candidates can be harder to recruit than in good times. Actively recruiting someone in a viable position is harder because there has to be a compelling reason for them to take your call. In addition to likely being overwhelmed (since they're the people doing all the work), passive candidates will be a lot more risk-averse. Thus, they will have less patience for your inquiry and will need to know a lot of information up front (this doesn't just apply to senior executives, but to lower level employees as well).

For instance, a passive candidate will likely want to know on the first call the risks, rewards, and the reasons they should consider making a move. They will definitely have a "show me the money" attitude. Before making the call, this requires that you talk to your Hiring Managers about a range of issues including compensation, severance, relocation, change in control and layoffs, and other "tools" for your toolbox. And when you make the call, it's important to be legitimately open and empathetic with candidates and to hear their concerns.

Candidate relocation, in particular, is a hard issue to deal with during this time, but with every challenge comes the opportunity to think out of the box and have more tools at your disposal for the future. Companies need to be prepared to pay more than they normally would for relocation. A candidate will typically not want to take a financial hit on their house. Some companies will guarantee a buyout of a house at its appraised value, and some will even offer more than the appraised value.

Another option is the hiring company can provide rental assistance for a candidate's current home. The company may help them find a renter while the candidate looks for a buyer and if they can't sell it in six months the company will buy it.

There are many variations for how to deal with this issue. The key here is to be open-minded and come up with creative solutions. It's also important to work with internal or external relocation experts to come up with options and then educate senior leadership on this issue.

Challenging job markets enable you to deepen and improve your relationships with third-party recruiting partners. Let's face it—we can't do everything ourselves. There's no reason you can't leverage your relationships with outside Recruiters for help in ways you hadn't before considered. And because they may be hurting too, many outside Recruiters will likely be more flexible in partnering with you.

For instance, many search firms will be more open to "unbundling" their services and perhaps discounting as well. But the key is to reach out to them and figure out a way to work together. And as with candidates, outside Recruiters will remember which companies reached out to them to find a way to work together during challenging times and those that never returned their call.

Thus challenging times are, in fact, opportunities for you to build your skills and relationships as a Recruiter that will enable you to continue to stand out from the pack, add value to your organization, and have greater tools at your disposal for when the tide turns and the good times roll in once again.

PROACTIVE RELATIONSHIP BUILDING

Of course, it's a cliché to say that Talent Acquisition is all about relationships. But it's a cliché because it's true. I don't mean relationships like the shallow Hollywood kiss-kiss type. I mean *real* relationships.

Why? I've talked so often about your value as a Talent Acquisition professional/Recruiter to the company you work for. This time I want to talk about your value to yourself and to the world at large. Because when it comes to that, for Recruiters, it's all about relationships.

What that means is your ability to go out and connect with people to get information you need, to give information to others so you preserve your pipeline and deal with difficult situations when conflict arises, and to get your job done and maintain your contacts. Right now, in the world of Talent Acquisition there's lots of talk about technology, tools, the power of the Internet, blah, blah, blah. That's all well and good, and I'll touch upon those tools in a recruiting context later, but the point is they're *tools*. Tools to get you to the most important thing: *talking and connecting with other people*. In the world of recruiting there is no substitute for the basics because there is one fact that is unalienable: great Recruiters—the ones who stand out and succeed—are great relationship builders.

Here's the thing about building relationships—you can't wait for them to come to you. Just because you're a "service provider" either inside or outside an organization doesn't mean you should wait for the service to come to you. The best internal Recruiters I have ever seen are the inquisitive, proactive ones, the ones who don't wait for the Hiring Managers to call. They pick up the phone and talk to people running the various businesses to understand the issues, goals, and objectives of their divisions.

You may respond, "How can we do that—we're too busy!" Well, it turns out that if you make time to do this you actually *save yourself* time later on because when the requisition comes in you already understand many elements of the need.

For example, I hired someone once whom I knew was a great Recruiter but had no experience in the business area in which she joined. She came in and made it her job to know that business on her own. She didn't wait for the requisition order; she sought out key people in operations to help her understand the business. She did a lot of this in the off hours. When she first started she would do this two or three times a week. Soon, not only was she well prepared to be a business partner to the managers, she became respected. She went on "their turf" and made the division managers comfortable ahead of time. Recruiters think they don't have time for this, but if they don't make time, they'll lose out on an opportunity to increase their value to the organization.

So whenever I talk about real relationships, not the kissy-kissy Hollywood ones, Recruiters always fidget uncomfortably because to deal with and develop relationships with any substance means to deal with conflict and difficult situations. Talent Acquisition professionals and Recruiters hate this because, as we all know, Recruiters like to be liked! By nature, Recruiters are not set up for conflict and confrontation. But we must get over this and disarm the big green scary monster over the hill. You know what I'm talking about.

Bad Relationships

There are two different types of bad relationships I'd like to address. The first are ones that we often times generate in the form of candidates whom we need to sign off; the second are those who have a negative bias toward recruiting inside of an organization.

Regarding the former, there was some myth created by someone in the 1970s (it had to be because they were old school) that says never give bad news to a candidate and instead tell them they won't be going any further in a search. This had to have been created by a Recruiter because only a Recruiter, in their desire to be liked, would avoid the possibility of conflict in this way (conflict, by the way, that only comes up perhaps five percent of the time). The truth is while many Recruiters don't follow up and close the loop with unsuccessful candidates, hoping to avoid conflict, this has the opposite effect of relationship building. It *alienates* former prospects. What Recruiters have to remember is that *every* time we talk to candidates it holds the potential for a possible relationship in the future. Candidates don't fall off the face of the earth, so it's vital that if they won't be going any further in a search, the Recruiter must *call* them (not send an e-mail or letter) to turn them down. All that needs to be said is that the Hiring Manager decided to pursue candidates he/she felt were more appropriate. If there is a specific skill set that's missing that can be mentioned too.

Here's one of my favorite experiences. I was hiring a Vice President of HR for a division of a large company I was with, and I had built a relationship with a candidate who interviewed and ultimately didn't get the job. Six months later there was another opening so I called the candidate again. He came in, went through the fifteen-interview process, and still didn't get the role. But each time he appreciated my honest and direct feedback in following up as to why he didn't get the role. He appreciated the candor. Eventually he moved on and got another job, and I moved on and did a variety of things as well. But we always kept in touch. When I started my consulting business many years ago I called him and he engaged me for a two-and-a-half year project—all because our relationship was based on how things were handled during his two unsuccessful attempts at joining my prior company.

The second type of bad relationship is a little trickier: dealing with those in your company who have a negative bias toward recruiting. In a literal sense this may not be a bad relationship because chances are you don't know them and they don't know you. It's more like a bad impression. But there is a way to turn this bad impression into a relationship tool and have it work to your benefit.

When I was at a technology company there were some who hated recruiting and others who loved it. There was one person in particular who was very talented as a technologist but a nasty screamer when it came to internal Talent Acquisition. Since this was an important person in the company, my job was to disarm him. How did I do that? I involved him.

I put together an internal advisory board where I brought together those who hated us the most with those who loved us the most and engaged them in a dialogue. I posed various questions to them, including, "What should we do to improve our standing? What would you need to see that would enhance our credibility?" Eventually the screamer stopped screaming long enough to give us his thoughts. We were already doing much of what was suggested, but that's not the point. Just by engaging him in dialogue we got him vested in the process. Eventually he ended up helping us solve the problem. After that he had some ownership in our Talent Acquisition efforts and eventually became an evangelist. But undoubtedly the best relationships are the ones you foster that benefit you both and that can help you achieve your end goal of becoming a business partner in the business and increasing your own personal value substantially. Here are some tips and tools for fostering good relationships:

- **It goes both ways!** Always remember that the networking game goes both ways. If you're looking for someone to help you build your network you have to be able to give something up to do that. It could be proactively helping them, but more likely it could be as simple as following up with them on the people to whom they referred you. Looking back with them to update them on the people they know. Follow up is the magical seed that sprouts in unexpected ways.

- **Keep your relationship contacts fresh and active.** Use a technology tool that has a category area where you can detail how you know someone. You can integrate that with your other tools, such as Plaxo, that help maintain your contact list.

- **Leverage social networking tools such as LinkedIn, Facebook, and Twitter, Instagram.** Even various Talent Acquisition-specific communities have great social networks such as ERE.net, but remember it's just a bunch of recruiting folks—make sure your networking both in recruiting as well as business leaders. They help you understand who in your network is connected to others. If you're just starting, you can begin with people in your own organization.

- **Keep in touch regularly with your key relationships.** If not by phone, then touch base by e-mail. Have a tickler file to regularly see how they're doing.

- **Birthday reminders.** There are many tools with a birthday reminder that allows you to input the birthdays of everyone you know and automatically send them a birthday e-mail on the special day. Such an e-mail is shockingly pleasant thing to get because it's so personal. I've had many people who've been wowed by that.

- **Spend time with other Recruiters in your network.** It doesn't have to be a formal event such as those offered by your local Talent Acquisition and HR association, the Talent Acquisition Management association, or of course the ERE Expos offered through ERE Media, SHRM, and other organizations. Those events are wonderful, but you don't have to wait for them—you can create your own. Form a roundtable or a simple "meet up" (visit www.meetup.com).

- **Engage with "them."** Lastly, engage with third-party outside Recruiters. They're well connected and can add value, but as with everything else, make sure you give for what you get and you get for what you give.

I have discussed two types of relationships that are key to any consultative Recruiter: the relationships you build within your company, especially with those who might be rivals or who might not understand how you bring value to the business, and relationships that you build with your universe of candidates. But many Recruiters may need to outsource at least a part of their operation, and this means that another key relationship is the one you have with your third-party Recruiters.

LOVE ACTUALLY: THE TRUE VALUE OF THIRD-PARTY RECRUITER RELATIONSHIPS

When I first joined a large, consumer-oriented company as head of Talent Acquisition, I *thought* my goal was to build an empire and rule over all of the Talent Acquisition land. After all, wasn't it my job to do everything? Wasn't I hired to save the company money by handling *all* Talent Acquisition? To go "outside" would've been a sign of weakness in my kingdom and a crack in my carefully constructed Talent Acquisition castle of power (sound familiar?). So that's what I did. I created a self-sufficient, functionally aligned internal Talent Acquisition group set up to handle everything. And by handling everything my value in the company would truly be realized!

Here's the reality of what happened:

No matter how efficient or comprehensive we were, we couldn't handle everything. When you factor in the geographical, level, and functional needs with the peaks and valleys of the business, the only way we could've possibly filled every need was to create a Talent Acquisition organization so cumbersome no company in their right mind would have funded it. So of course, we had to turn to outside help and use third-party Recruiters (TPRs).

But here's the real kicker with my lemon strategy. Because we were located in our corporate offices, most of the Talent Acquisition we did was for the IT, finance, and administrative back-office stuff, not the stuff that was core to our business (Marketing, Engineering, and General Management). Why? Because the people who ran IT, Finance, and Administration were in offices right next door, could pop in frequently, and they tended to do so at their leisure with their inquiring presence as to the status of their searches.

Since the squeaky wheel gets the grease, we found ourselves responding to their inquiries and dedicating our resources to their work. But those weren't the jobs that were most important to the company, jobs on which we should've been focused. Since our resources were diverted elsewhere, we ended up assigning those key jobs to TPRs.

My value was not being realized. In fact, I had to fight for it to not go down.

Part of the problem was that even though my group couldn't handle everything I had already declared to anyone who would listen that our goal was to personally handle it all. I had staked my claim and was determined to live up to it. But this only resulted in a negative "push-pull" feeling internally. Because my team couldn't provide support, my "you have to use us" approach ended up alienating some of our internal clients; instead of providing reassurance, it gave them *incentive* to go around us and use outside Recruiter/TPRs on their own. And as I mentioned, because of capacity issues I wasn't handling the jobs most important to the company.

So what happened? In building my empire, where did I go awry?

I forgot what my job was. Worse, I forgot what represented true value to the company in someone like me (no wonder my value was suffering! My poor value…).

I thought my job (and thus the way for me to be most valuable) was to *do* everything. It wasn't. It was to make sure everything *got done*. It was to be a partner to my internal clients, not the whipping boy.

Why did I think I had to do everything? Because of cost, that's why. But the reality is when you can't do everything (and in the more than 30 years that I've been in this profession I've never seen a Talent Acquisition organization that could do it all, so let's just get past that one and move on), when you factor in the time savings (because you're bogged down with other stuff) and the quality of the results, using outside help is very cost-effective.

All of this is a long way of saying when your job is to be a strategic partner as a Talent Acquisition/HR professional and to ensure everything gets done. The goal is to be as valuable as possible, and cultivating successful relationships with TPRs is one of the most important things you can ever do.

So how do you begin? Well, not coincidentally, the key to success here as well is partnership, and this is the responsibility of both the HR/Talent Acquisition professional and TPR. Partnerships, as has been implied above, are based on trust and mutual respect. So to get to the land of respect and trust we have to address a little history.

Historically, there hasn't been a lot of trust and respect between HR/Talent Acquisition professionals and TPRs. Third-party Recruiters have tried to work with HR/Talent Acquisition but get shot down. So they have had to make their way around the HR/Talent Acquisition executive if they were going to get any search work. Conversely, during the times when HR/Talent Acquisition is involved in a search, Recruiter/TPRs have looked upon them as getting in the way and as a road block.

But in order for there to be a partnership, everybody's got to get past the past! Everybody's got to recognize that we're all in this for the support of our businesses and for our true values.

Why a partnership versus a transactional relationship? Because it's in everybody's best interests, that's why. From a Recruiter/TPR's perspective, a partnership means more of a consultative relationship and a steadier stream of work (for some reason, one of the "secrets" that Recruiter/TPRs (generally) don't get is there is a lot of work to be acquired through HR/Staffing). From the HR/Talent Acquisition perspective, partnerships with third-party Recruiters can directly affect cost, quality, reliability, and speed (having a partnership in place when you need to assign a search externally enables things to go so much quicker).

Okay, I really want my value to increase. How do I start?

The first step is for the HR/Talent Acquisition professional to recognize what the demand is internally for Talent Acquisition overall and, as part of that, the demand for third-party search work. This analysis is important for two reasons:

1) It requires close contact with Hiring Managers to not only assess where the business is going and near and long-term (18 months) needs but to identify the roles themselves and their importance.

2) Knowing the importance of the roles can help you determine which you want to do yourself and which you want to contract out.

Next, both parties need to work on the issue of respect and mutual trust. It's been my experience that in the history of the fissure that's formed in this area, HR/Talent Acquisition professionals have a little bit more to overcome in the eyes of Recruiter/TPRs than vice versa. So, I recommend the following:

- For HR/Talent Acquisition to sit with Recruiter/TPRs and reveal what the demand is for third-party search work, to give him or her a sense for the potential of the partnership. Tell them they won't get every search, but it gives them a sense that this is worth their time and efforts.

- Both parties can put together an informal service level agreement, which lays out generally how each party will work together. This can be done through e-mail.

- Lastly, on the issue of mutual respect and trust, both HR/Talent Acquisition professional and Recruiter/TPR need to acknowledge the value that each can bring to a partnership.

For HR/Talent Acquisition the value to be recognized is:

A. Enhanced access to company decision makers.

B. Broad details about the company culture.

C. An unbiased viewpoint to pre-sort candidates and prospects.

D. Smoothing over problems and issues between the Recruiter/TPR and Hiring Manager (the HR/Talent Acquisition person needs to ensure that if there's a problem with one Recruiter/TPR, the Hiring Manager doesn't ban the whole search firm; relationships are not with firms but with search professionals, and there are other areas of the firm that can still be used).

E. Helping to speed things along and facilitating the work of a TPR versus being a roadblock (an internal HR/Talent Acquisition person can walk documents over to the Hiring Manager).

For the Recruiter/TPR the value to be recognized is:

A. Recognizing HR/Talent Acquisition can add value.

B. Identifying the internal HR/Talent Acquisition person as an advocate from whom can get more business, not less.

C. Acknowledging that HR/Talent Acquisition is the "client" as much as any Hiring Manager; they are not separate.

D. Letting go of any issues regarding "ownership of candidates"—if you keep in mind the overall goal of partnership it doesn't matter who identified the successful candidate. The overall goal is quality and speed.

E. Recognizing that the better you make HR/Talent Acquisition look internally and the more you help them realize their value, the better you will be looked upon by HR/Talent Acquisition and the more work they will want to give you!

There are several specific ways in which partnerships between HR/ Talent Acquisition and TPRs can be formed, as well as certain things that can be done to foster those partnerships.

Service level agreements are a good way to start.

An annual Recruiter/TPR summit is a success practice technique in which you bring all of your trusted Talent Acquisition partners together and "open the kimono" so to speak. You sit and talk with them about company strategy and give them information on your top-line demand analysis. Recruiter/ TPRs also get a chance to see their competition. But if they know your company strategy and feel like trusted consultants, they can *always* be proactively on the lookout for candidates for you. And it adds to their feeling like a true strategic partner.

Preferred provider relationships can be a very effective way to consolidate the best Talent Acquisition firms with the positions you will need filled. The best preferred provider arrangements are not only about price but rather are set up to create incentives for quality and results. However, HR/Talent Acquisition professionals need to be careful of the complacent flip side of these situations—preferred provider relationships can be a crutch to not continuing to renew the Recruiter/TPR relationship pipeline and consider others who can do it better and faster. You should always consider trying new firms. If it's on contingency, why not?

Recruiter/TPRs can provide help to HR/Talent Acquisition executives in ways other than pure recruiting. For example, say an HR/Talent Acquisition professional is looking to create a position profile. The position is new, so they're in search of a template. As a Recruiter/TPR, going out of your way to provide them with one and make their life easier goes a long way toward making the HR/Talent Acquisition professional feel like *they* have a trusted partner, not just a search person.

HR/Talent Acquisition professionals need to stop placing Recruiter/TPRs in the same corporate bucket as purchasing/procurement/vendor services. In other words, if you strike a deal with a recruitment firm it shouldn't go through purchasing all by itself—HR/Talent Acquisition needs to be engaged. They should be considered as a partner, not a vendor.

Finally, both parties need to recognize that there's value when TPR call HR/Talent Acquisition professionals out of the blue. The HR/ Talent Acquisition professional should treat "intrusiveness" as something that works for you. Being dismissive isn't smart or appropriate and just getting materials isn't as helpful as meeting in person. Recognize that a Recruiter/TPR's world (and yours for that matter) is all about personal relationships. Give them a shot but set boundaries. And TPRs need to recognize and respect those boundaries.

Ultimately, the relationships between HR/Talent Acquisition, Recruiter/TPRs, and the candidate pool can and should be mutually beneficial. If everyone can recognize the value of true partnerships, all will see their own individual professional value skyrocket. And then there truly will be love all around. Now that we have established a framework for the "macro" relationships that must be created among these key constituents, let's zoom in on the sometimes delicate process that creates the "micro" relationship between the Recruiter and the individual candidate. The nurturing of individual relationships, forged during the interview process, will bring value to your Talent Acquisition brand.

Let's look at some familiar interview situations.

INTERVIEWING STORIES AND WHAT WE LEARN FROM THEM

Like many of you, I've have had many interesting experiences interviewing candidates. If you think about it, the candidate interview is a unique experience—that strange dance between two strangers, one human being sitting across from another, asking them about their life and accomplishments with an eye toward assessing if they are a fit for a particular role. I guess one of the great things about human nature is our unpredictability. You don't know what's going to come out of the other person's mouth or how the experience will end up. How many of us have gone in with high expectations of an individual based on their experience on paper only to be let down? Conversely, who of us hasn't had that rush of excitement when a candidate unexpectedly turns out to be a winner, surprising us at every turn with their responses and reaffirming our belief in what we do as Recruiters and Talent Acquisition professionals? It's a setup that never fails to produce interesting outcomes.

Let me preface this by saying I am not an interviewing guru. I don't sell my interviewing process in training sessions, books, or other products. The purpose of this is not to produce a best practices approach to interviewing. Rather, as someone who has done a lot of interviews (as a former corporate head of

Talent Acquisition and Recruiting, and currently as a Talent Acquisition and Recruitment Process Optimization Consultant), I thought there might be some things to learn from the following stories. In other words, maybe you'll laugh, maybe you'll cry, maybe you'll snicker, but maybe, like me, you'll learn something as well.

The Restaurant Interview

During my time in Talent Acquisition for a consumer company we had a search for a Vice President of Marketing. There was a woman who ran marketing for a big restaurant chain whom my bosses (clients), the operational heads of the company, were particularly keen to recruit. This executive had attracted a lot of "buzz" because of her recent accomplishments and bold marketing initiatives. After several attempts to contact her, the woman finally agreed to meet with me, but she would not travel to our city to interview. Knowing how important this was to my internal clients, I flew to her city and interviewed her in one of her local restaurants.

The interview seemed to go well and I remember thinking, "Hmm, my bosses were right. She's solid." We talked about next steps, and I had mentioned we would want her to fly to our company to meet with my bosses/clients. That's when the conversation took an interesting turn:

Me: "We'd like to fly you out to meet with some additional executives in our company. We're very interested in proceeding."
Her: "I'd be interested in that."
Me: "Great!"
Her: "I'd be happy to meet with you and your company further, but our meeting would have to be in one of the local outlets of this restaurant chain."
Me: "Excuse me?"
Her: "I said I can only meet you in one of our restaurants in your city."
Me: "Why?"
Her: "Because the world is a dirty place, there are germs everywhere, and I don't trust cleanliness, food, or service anywhere but in one of our restaurants."
Me: "You can't be serious."
Her: "I'm completely serious."

Okay. The problem was my bosses had already prejudged her favorably and were sold on her!

When I returned from my trip, I had to take a pretty hard stand with my business leaders. Even before we called her, they had convinced themselves they needed to hire this person. Even though it was my job to snag her, I now had to convince them that she was not going to be a culture fit.

It was a tense situation, but I stood my ground. Ultimately, they agreed.

Lesson: what I learned was that as a Talent Acquisition professional and Recruiter, taking a stand to protect our company's business by *not* hiring someone is as important as trying to snag an élite person.

The Hotel Interview

I once worked for a hotel company where we offered candidates the ability to fill out applications that had a short essay about why you wanted to work for our company. We had created an open, walk-in interview schedule whereby anyone could submit an application, and we would interview anyone who had applied.

A guy came in and filled out the application and was very earnest in his desire to work for the company. My colleague interviewed him, and he seemed like a congenial, straightforward individual. It was a busy day for us all, and we didn't have time to thoroughly review every application before beginning the interview. Thus, during the interview, my colleague turned over the application to the back, which included the short essay about why you were interested in working for the company, and read the following:

I have spent the last several years as a male escort/prostitute. I have recently turned my life around and found God. I am looking for a real job, something more stable and with a healthy future. When I was considering all the companies I might want to work for, I immediately thought of this hotel. I have done a substantial amount of business here (for which I hope you will accept my sincerest apologies) and always found it to be an incredibly nice place. It would be an honor to work here.

Lesson: as strange as this was for my colleague and me, we really appreciated the fact that this individual was straightforward with us. Though he didn't get the job, we were very open and honest with him about why. It underscored the value to me of being open and accepting yet honest about what is appropriate and what isn't.

The Anxiety Interview

When I was head of Talent Acquisition for a large entertainment company, we were doing a search for a particularly difficult role. There was an individual whom we knew we wanted and was very appropriate for the role, but it was impossible to get through to him. We tried to reach him for weeks and finally did. Even then he was reluctant to talk to us. He had worked for the same company for 15 years and was really not interested in making a move. Nonetheless, we persisted, and begged and pleaded with him to give us an opportunity to talk with him. Finally, he relented and agreed to come in for an interview.

He had mentioned at the outset that throughout his career he had never had to formally interview. I didn't think too much about this, and the interview began typically enough with questions about his life and professional experience.

Almost from the very beginning this individual shifted in his seat uncomfortably. Soon he began to sweat. Not perspire, but Albert-Brooks-in-*Broadcast-News* sweat. Right in the middle of a response to one of my questions, he popped up, grabbed a folder from my desk and started fanning himself, talking all the time.

I asked if he was all right. He said he was fine.

We continued our conversation, but his discomfort only increased. It began to make *me* uncomfortable. Finally, I asked if he wanted to take a break and go to the restroom, and he did.

Forty minutes later, there was still no word from him. Finally, realizing something had gone seriously wrong, I sent someone in to check on him. Apparently, he was a wreck. He had thrown up all over the place and had become overcome with anxiety. We offered to help him any way we could and set it up so he could excuse himself discreetly through the back door.

Lesson 1: I think that our problems with this individual began when we tried too hard to develop him as a candidate. If someone is very reluctant at the outset, there are usually reasons for that. Bottom line, at the end of the day, it doesn't serve anyone well to persuade someone to do what they really don't want to do. We also could have done a better job of prescreening this individual on the phone.

Lesson 2: When we followed up with this individual, he was very grateful for the way we handled this very awkward situation. We kept in touch and on a separate assignment he ended up giving us a referral that was very helpful. It reminded me how important it is to treat those we interview with respect and how they do not go away. I can't tell you how often I've bumped into people in my personal life whom I interviewed in the past for a particular role.

The Remote Interview

Nowadays, people participate in video interviews, or can send in pre-recorded responses to a set of questions. I shared the stories of some industries who demand a certain look or physical attribute for their organization, and this is a good way to get a feel for an individual before you meet them in person. While this can also cause anxiety for candidates, it can also yield some interesting interview footage. I've heard of candidates doing video from some interesting places including; bathrooms of their current employer, in their cars while commuting (not very safe!), and one of my personal favorites, from their bed, including wearing a bathrobe. While this candidate was very competent, it seems she forgot that video has both a visual and an audio component. It was difficult not to be distracted by her fuzzy pink robe and the notion that she decided interviewing in her pajamas might've been a good idea.

Lesson 1: While there is a level of appreciation for candidates who are interviewing while they have a current role, and perhaps, no private space to interview, the bathroom is not an ideal spot. While it's far more stressful for people to show up at an office, sometimes, people even senior in their careers do not have a lot of experience interviewing and can make interesting judgement calls

Lesson 2: If you interview in your bathrobe, you will become a legend or anecdote for all time. I can't tell you how many times the story of this woman confidently sharing her experience in her robe comes up as a cautionary tale.

Miscellaneous

We all have several small experiences that stick in our minds. I once was wooing a well-respected Recruiter from a competitor and took him to lunch at a casual dining restaurant. During the course of our interview, he proceeded to order a massive lunch. It was enough food for a family of 6 and that struck me as odd, but I chalked it up to, "I guess he has a big appetite and maybe eats his main meal at lunch."

The problem was he ate a normal-sized meal and carried the bulk of his food out in doggie bags. It was obvious that he had just done his weekly grocery shopping at my expense.

And lastly, I once had an executive-level candidate show up for an interview in my office with a T-shirt that read "Jesus Is My Homey."

The bottom line is that we've all had experiences in interviews where people act strangely. It's part of the joy of this job and the unpredictability of human nature. But when that happens, here are some tips to remember:

- Remember that the interview is an inherently unnatural situation.

- No matter how awkward, always treat people with respect and dignity.

- In certain types of roles, especially technical ones, star performers can be bad interviewers.

- Individuals who have been with the same company for a long time may not be well practiced in their interviewing skills.

- It's not what the interview subject does, it's how you handle it.

- Document experiences with strange interview situations.

- If someone does something peculiar or odd in an interview, consider it one data point that can be explored further during the referencing process (assuming it's not *too* peculiar or odd).

And above all, remember that in the end we're all just human beings and when two human beings get together to do the "interview dance" anything can happen.

Now that I have covered the basics of candidate relations, including the need to communicate fairly and effectively with all prospects and how to conduct interviews, let's drill deeper into how the Recruiter needs to effectively manage every aspect of the candidate relationship.

THE CANDIDATE'S PERSPECTIVE

One of the best things you can do to understand candidate relations is to put yourself in the candidate's shoes. After all, they are the ones who are putting themselves out there; they are opening up their lives for your inspection. As a consultative Recruiter you need to perform due diligence and get the information you need to make an informed decision. During this process you can either make a friend of the candidate or make an enemy. It is entirely your choice. You can do your job and even deliver bad news in a way that is respectful and enhances the brands of you and your company.

You make an impression that can last forever. Once the interview process is over, what do you want candidates to say about you?

How about this: "So few companies even asked this question or seemed to care." Or: "I didn't get the job, but the people there were very nice and gave me a chance."

From the candidates' perspective, here is what they could love about applying for a job at your company—and what they could hate.

The Top Nine Things That Candidates Love (drum roll, please):

1. Being treated with respect at every level, even if they are not the final candidate.

2. Getting help resigning from their current employer and being given flexibility regarding their start date with their new job.

3. Being asked for feedback about the interviews and the hiring process.

4. Having open and honest communication about objections to their history.

5. Getting a list of information they would have to provide prior to an offer.

6. Having someone help them with the application process, if they need help.

7. Getting courtesy telephone calls about the status of their candidacy.

8. Participating in a transparent interview process.

9. Talking to people who are knowledgeable about their background.

The Top Ten Things That Candidates Hate:

1. Not getting feedback or status communication on the status of their interviews.

2. Going through an interview process only to find out that the job is not really open.

3. Enduring background checks that find issues out of their control.

4. Having to go through a gauntlet of unnecessary interviews on multiple days.

5. Feeling as if they are the perfect candidate for the job but can't get an interview.

6. Dealing with interviewers who are unprepared or never even read their resume.

7. Having to navigate a difficult or invasive application process (usually online).

8. Learning that someone on the interview team questioned their resume.

9. Dealing with unprofessional and condescending HR professionals.

10. Not knowing the interview logistics (who, what, where, and why) in advance.

These are the same things that you would love or hate if you were applying for a job.

Some HR professionals are not "wired" to think about the candidate. Often, there is a belief that unsuccessful candidates simply go away like the people in the old *Twilight Zone* episode who were sent to the cornfield, never to be seen again. Unlike the poor souls in the *Twilight Zone*, candidates don't go away. Candidates live in our communities. You may see a candidate at your kid's soccer game or at the supermarket.

If we don't provide respectful feedback or information on status it is because we may feel as if candidates will "just get the message." So in our minds, there is no need to have a confrontation with unsuccessful candidates.

But your personal brand and your own personal reputation as a person are at stake. The "golden rule" is often forgotten.

Remember the story of Faberge shampoo? It's all about viral communications: "I'll tell two friends, and so on, and so on, and so on." In addition to telling their friends, co-workers, colleagues, and family members about their experiences, they have other ways to spread both the good and bad news.

There are several online communities that allow candidates to provide their feedback about the interviewing and candidate experience, including Glassdoor.com and WetFeet.com (primarily for university hires). Check them out.

In a tough economy we cannot forget that there is a cost of bad candidate experiences. Future candidate sourcing costs are impacted. It could take longer to source quality candidates. Your company/consumer brand can be negatively impacted. HR and Hiring Manager relationships could drive negative reactions in the future.

Don't hesitate to ask the candidate for his or her opinion of the process. You may get bitterness, but you may also get real insights. If we do not ask candidates about their experience, we will never know what they are saying. Never assume.

Tell candidates at the beginning of the process that you will ask their opinions. Ask candidates throughout the process for their feedback. Ask candidates at the conclusion of the process, no matter what the outcome was. If you do ask for feedback, make sure you follow up on suggestions.

Candidate Surveys

As I reviewed in our discussion on metrics earlier in this book, candidate surveys are critical. Having surveys helps us get excellent, unbiased, and consistent feedback. Simply asking for feedback after the process does not allow for unbiased and consistent feedback. There should be at least three different types of candidate surveys:

1. Candidates who interviewed in person for the job, but did not get an offer.

2. Candidates who interviewed in person for the job and were offered a job, but declined the offer.

3. Newly hired employees.

Some organizations have created separate surveys for university candidates, executive candidates, and online applicants. Surveys should be sent out in e-mail not later than once a quarter (make sure you collect e-mail addresses at the beginning of the process). Tell candidates you will send a survey to gather their feedback. A great way to ensure a prompt response for the surveys is to provide an incentive such as a drawing (you can do this quarterly) for something small, like a gift card or, if your company has consumer-oriented products, something from your company.

Use simple and free survey tools such as SurveyMonkey, Zoomerang, or other survey tools. If you have an ATS system, you can simply export the proper e-mails directly from the system.

Candidate Expectations

Remember, all candidates have expectations. Only you can meet the expectations of your candidates. Always tell candidates what to expect about the process and when to expect it. Always follow through with these commitments. If you don't have an answer, call them anyways.

Most HR pros are not wired to say "no" effectively. Often there is a fear of confrontation. We must not avoid our responsibility and must ensure that we are able to maintain personal and professional dignity and the dignity of those we say "no" to.

In most cases, we really don't use the word "no" outright. We can express ourselves professionally using different words. Triangulate your conversations by talking about the issue or problem and not making the conversation about the other party. Remove the word "you" from your conversation—take out the personalization.

When you feel the need to challenge a particular position, make sure you are prepared with research or facts from your own experience. This will keep the exchange as separated as it can be from being about you, or them. If you are very passionate about the topic at hand, take the time to formulate the argument before engaging in a discussion.

When Telling a Candidate "No"

There are ways to deliver your message clearly yet tactfully. Consider using the appropriate response: "We have decided to pursue candidates whose background and qualifications more suit the position at this time." If candidates ask why, usually repeating this statement is enough.

If it's appropriate, you can offer BFOQ (bona-fide occupational qualification) oriented responses such as, "The position requires a strong working knowledge of SAP and we're not confident that you are ready for what we need." Feel free to use technology (such as e-mail) to respond and automate the response process to candidates who respond to your job postings and submit resumes.

Do *not* use e-mail to reject candidates who have interviewed in person for a position. E-mail rejection is cowardly and unprofessional. Always call on the phone. Use the phone to help build and drive solid candidate relationships.

Always call candidates who interviewed in person directly to update them on the status of their candidacy. Never leave a voicemail message with the status (good or bad) of their candidacy. Simply leave a neutral voicemail that asks them to call you back.

As a Talent Acquisition consultant, you need to build your value to the organization. Recruiters who are valued are those who "get it" and who can clearly and credibly communicate how the business operates and what it takes to be successful inside the organization. Recruiters are valued who contract well, live up to their side of the bargain, and have built, constantly refresh, and maintain solid outside networks of talent that may benefit the organization in the future.

Make sure you understand how to connect the process of Talent Acquisition to the rest of the HR organization (such as linking recruiting with talent development). Focus on being a consultant, not a customer-service person. Focus on building strong relationship skills both internally and externally (and not just with other Recruiters).

Try out and measure all tools and resources that may be available to you. Don't use technology as a crutch—nothing will replace the power of a phone call with a real live person!

Ask your candidates about the hiring process. Remember that most of your competitors don't bother asking candidates who were not offered a job. Have solid data on *talent* competitors, not just *industry* competitors, and their employment propositions. Make sure your contact pipeline data is up to date and critical.

Use the tools available to leverage technology to help.

At the end of the day, all the wonderful technological tools aside, it is all about relationships. And the key to great relationship building, as in most things in life, is to do it before you need it. Having relationships before you need to harvest them will enable you to always stay one step ahead, and in this day and age, that'll separate you from the pack, build your own personal value, and make you one of best.

MANAGING YOUR EMPLOYER BRAND

Every time you interact with a candidate you create an impression. When the process is over the candidate may walk away thinking, "Wow, what a great company—if they had another opening I'd apply there again." Or the candidate may think, "What a bunch of jerks. I'd never want to work there." Now multiply these impressions dozens or even hundreds of times. This is a powerful force. This is your professional brand.

By definition, branding is a means of identifying and differentiating a company, product, or service. Branding includes the tangibles and intangibles: features, services, and benefits that create and influence an ongoing relationship. It is the development of an affinity for a product that in turn takes on elevated meaning and a predisposition to buy/join. A brand is a set of convictions that surrounds a product/service/job in the consumer's (job seekers/employees) mind. Effective branding creates a sustainable competitive advantage. Negative branding can damage your ability to reach your goals.

How can we apply this to the employment experience? What goals can we set? Why should we use employer branding anyway?

The fact is you have no choice. With every candidate interview you are *creating* your brand; you just may not be *managing* your brand. How can we manage our employer brand? We need to take the messages that best focus what we are, where we want to go, how we can get there, and who will help us. We need to communicate those messages and cement them into all our exchanges with people externally and internally.

What are the goals of an employer brand?

- Express the nature of our company.

- Differentiate us from competitors.

- Work across all forms of communication.

- Work within the overall company brand.

- Add value to the overall brand.

- Get the right candidates into the pipeline.

- Gain respect and build morale from employees already employed.

Branding Tools

What do organizations have to work with in managing their employer brand? They include the company name, logo, and other trademarks, and the individual brands of products and services offered. It's the general sense of the work environment and the public perception of the company. Branding is created with cross-marketing channels (do we hire George Clooney, or Serena Williams to be our spokesperson). The company brand can show where the organization is headed.

The brand management process is how brand development proceeds from the first task—asset assessment—through five stages to emerge as the organizations' brand expression in the marketplace:

1. **Asset Assessment.** Be honest: what are your strengths and weaknesses? How large is your company—do you need people who thrive in an intense corporate environment, or do you want people who are happy to have a more stable career? What benefits do you offer? Is there opportunity for advancement?

2. **Employee Involvement.** What is your organizational culture? Is it vertical, with top-down direction with little front-line input, or are decisions made on a broad collaborative basis? Is there opportunity for creative thinking?

3. **Competitive Assessment.** What other organizations can your candidates work for? You need to know who your competitors are and what they offer. If another company offers higher wages, can you compensate with profit sharing or better benefits?

4. **Brand Positioning.** You need to know where your organization fits in the overall market. Does your company compete on price, like Walmart, or are you targeting the Cartier upscale market? Are you known for promoting from within? Does your company have a reputation for treating women and minorities fairly?

5. **Brand Expression.** This is the combined effect of all of the "brand signals" that are present in the marketplace and are picked up by consumers and candidates. Every element of your Talent Acquisition

brand needs to be in alignment. For example, if you claim to provide equal opportunity for every race, creed, and gender, you'd better make sure that candidates who walk into your offices see employees of different races, creeds, and genders.

For the consultative Recruiter, the mission is to fill the organizational pipeline with qualified candidates. What do you have to work with? The answer depends upon the combination of everything that goes into the brand management process. Let's take a look at one example.

Case Study: Idealab

Founded in Pasadena, California, in 1996, Idealab is a company that creates and operates pioneering technology companies. The project is to create a brand management process that expresses the nature of Idealab and differentiates Idealab from competitors. It should work across all media and add value to the overall brand. For this project, employee input was a key component. Internal focus groups were composed of a cross section of employees including technical, nontechnical, new hires, old- timers, etc.

Asset Assessment

Idealab brand assets include the Idealab name, individual company names/logos-brands, Idealab employees having a general sense of a good work environment, and a unique compensation menu (take your pick between high equity/lower salary or vice versa).

The focus groups provided information on where people had come from, what had prompted them to leave elsewhere, and what they were looking for. The group also discussed what had brought them to Idealab, how that experience has lived up to expectations, and what would keep them there.

It was learned that *in other companies* where staff had worked, the work was boring, staff members were underpaid, underappreciated, underutilized, and treated like "peons" by too many "suits" and unpleasant managers. There was an overall feeling of disenfranchisement. Outside of the company, there was a disconnect between anything they did and anything that happened.

Idealab was positioned as a company where there was responsibility, respect, empowerment, and trust. *The opportunity to make things happen* became the employer brand positioning. The branding campaign built on top of the positioning would have to expand upon the themes of responsibility and empowerment expressed in the tagline; retain a clean and orderly appearance to work within the Idealab brand and to reflect the order of thinking and break through the clutter of standard promises, bulleted facts, and self-conscious attempts to look hip.

"I Will"

In the "I" campaign, the opportunity to make something happen expressed in the tagline becomes the obligation to make something happen, expressed in the phrase, "I will."

Graphically in the "I" campaign the "I" is always surrounded by enough free space to allow ideas to happen. Within that space is room for the individual initiative and imagination that is directly connected to the success of our ideas.

CONCLUSION

In today's competitive global economy, even during periods of high unemployment when there is a surplus of active candidates, woe unto the consultative Recruiter who takes his or her job for granted.

Your professional goal is twofold: to place the best possible candidate in every open position and to ensure that your pipeline is producing a steady stream of qualified candidates. To do this—especially when the economy heats up and unemployment rates go down—you must create and manage two sets of brands: your company's external brand in the minds of potential candidates and the internal brand of your consultative Talent Acquisition group.

This requires a high level of professionalism and ethics both in how you interact with your individual candidates (those whom you hire and those whom you do not hire) and how you interact with the company, its executives, and its Hiring Managers.

You live in a 360-degree world of relationships. As a consultative Recruiter, you need to create and nurture positive relationships with stakeholders including your pool of job candidates, HR Generalists in your company, Hiring Managers, and third-party Recruiters. Some of these relationships may seem competitive or even adversarial; in others, you hold power that you must use wisely. In every case, openness, high ethical standards, and a positive attitude will help you build your personal brand and enhance your career.

CHAPTER 10: CHANGE MANAGEMENT

At the many HR and Recruiting conferences and networking sessions that I attend, the issue that I find most important is rarely addressed: leading and managing change. This is probably one of the most essential skills a Talent Acquisition or HR leader should have in their toolkit.

In our communities we're constantly coming up with great ideas about *initiating change,* but all of that is worthless unless we can execute and implement those ideas. Because we have to change and flex every minute of the day, planning for good and difficult times alike requires excellent change management skills. And as someone who has learned some hard lessons over the course of my career in not knowing how to manage change, I write from experience.

For instance, when I was head of Talent Acquisition for a large, multi-billion-dollar company, the entire organization participated in a global reengineering initiative. In HR, we decided to take advantage of this effort to implement some changes of our own. We decided to combine all of the Talent Acquisition functions in the separate business units into a centralized, shared-services model. As the leader of the Talent Acquisition area I figured that since the whole company was going through change there was no need to have any *additional* communication with our clients about our Talent Acquisition reorganization—after all, it could be considered as simply another element of what we were all going through.

It wasn't until the head of HR of a business unit and my boss were sitting in my office complaining about my team's dwindling performance in the wake of this change that I realized just how important it is to communicate extensively about, and have a comprehensive plan for, implementing change.

It's not that I didn't communicate at all about what was happening; it's that I didn't "get it" in terms of what was necessary with respect to engaging others and making them partners with me in this change. I was subjecting my plan to what we like to call "death by PowerPoint"—I was going around with my little PowerPoint presentation tucked under my arm informing everyone as to what was *going to happen* versus *truly engaging and communicating* with them. Though the change was ultimately implemented, the cost was high—

people we wanted to keep within our Talent Acquisition organization left and some of our customers were alienated.

WHEN SARAH MEETS SALY

The first step in this process is to realize that whenever change is involved there's always something called SALY in the room. SALY stands for "Same As Last Year." SALY is that urge in all of us (in some stronger than others) to resist change. It's the urge to say "Let's stick with what we did last year;" to cling to the familiar, the comfortable. So, before anything happens it's always important to realize SALY's in the room.

However, knowing this can help you frame a strategy for implementing change. It's important to understand how people deal with change. My experience is that, though everyone deals with change differently, people generally meet change with the reaction I called SARAH (Shock, Anger, Resistance, Acceptance, and Help).

So what are some guidelines for leading people through change? The fact is that not having an effective change management plan is usually the death of projects. Organizations involved in global Talent Acquisition are constantly changing environments in which new processes are rolled out regularly. At many organizations change is so frequent that they adopt global change management programs. But even that isn't enough. For each change you need to have a specific change plan and internal and external change communications plans. Without those in place, it is not only confusing for everyone, but it ends up costing the company money.

So in order to manage change, we have to have at least one and perhaps several change management plans. (This was the beginning of the mistakes I made in my scenario earlier. Since I figured our change would be part of the larger change plan, I did not feel the need to create a separate one for us in Talent Acquisition).

Because change in an area as vital as Talent Acquisition effects so many, it really can't be successfully implemented without a plan. An effective change management plan will focus on many levels (the broad as well as the specific) and will include an emphasis on everything from the organization to your team to individuals. In fact, the act of putting together the plan will be enormously helpful because it will not only require identifying who the stakeholders are and who will be affected, but it will also require strategizing how to approach and engage them in the implementation.

Importantly, having a plan will enable you to plan for mistakes, which is a vital and valuable part of any new venture. How will a plan give you the opportunity to make mistakes? Because the cornerstone, foundation, and lifeblood of any change management plan is perhaps the most vital element in the whole change management scenario: communication.

When starting up a corporate Talent Acquisition function, engage people *from the very beginning.* By using focus groups, you can get people involved who are going to be affected and share your vision and proposed process as well as help you figure out how to really make it work. It is critical to engage stakeholders and then communicate, monitor, and adjust your process continuously. It's a constant process of educating Hiring Managers, HR partners, and key business leaders and getting feedback.

When communicating, try to mix it up and be entertaining so that people remain interested. During your focus group meetings, use interactive voting devices to keep the audience engaged in answering questions and giving feedback. In your rollout of the new process, make a video showing the recruiting process in action with a touch of humor to keep it fresh. In your monthly written communication, hide a question related to the recruiting marketplace and give a prize to the first few people who answer it. You can also use a "Myth Of The Month" whereby you debunk the latest myths that have surfaced with respect to the new processes. Through the use of Hiring Manager and candidate surveys you can constantly monitor to determine what is or isn't working properly and then adjust accordingly.

But sometimes even that level of communication isn't enough. You know that old rule of when you pack for a trip you lay out all your clothes and then take away half? Change management communication is the *opposite* of that. No matter how much you plan to communicate with respect to change management you should take that plan and double it.

Why is this important? Whatever the change is you're implementing, it's not about it being a good or right idea—it's about bringing everyone along with you. One of the things people in Talent Acquisition management often don't understand about communications is that it's not just about making sure you and your ideas are *heard*, it's about making sure everyone is *with* you. It's a bit of a paradox—in order to do what you want to do you need to focus less on that and more on the communication needs of those affected. Because in the end that will help you get to where you want to go. You need to focus on what your clients and stakeholders need to hear and know so that they'll arrive at where you want them to be.

This approach underscores yet another mistake I made in my scenario above: I was so focused on communicating my change and ensuring I was heard that I didn't focus on the communication needs of my clients and stakeholders.

When it comes to managing change, there is nothing more important than communication. And with a change management plan, constant communication gives you the room to make mistakes.

In summary, here are some guidelines for leading people through change.

- Prepare for the change before it occurs.

- Provide a clear description of the change and a picture of success.

- Find and remove obstacles before the change occurs.

- Allow adequate time for people to accept the change.

- Involve affected people in planning the change.

- Provide motivation for people to embrace the change.

- Find and utilize resources and people that support the change.

- Allow the change to be shaped by ongoing feedback.

- Provide clear implementation objectives for all people involved in the change.

- Continually monitor the change and adjust resource levels.

- Reinforce the new behaviors through formal and informal methods.

- View leading others through change as an ongoing process.

Remember, though there are a thousand great ideas out there, only when you've created and successfully *executed* a plan (and SARAH has met SALY!) will you have developed perhaps the most important skill that a Talent Acquisition and HR manager can possess.

Change can come from within your organization, but just as often it is imposed from the outside environment—such as during a recession.

REAL UPSIDE FROM AN INGLORIOUS DOWNTURN

There's no question the global recession that emerged in late 2008 was difficult and a game changer for Recruiters. Not only were there far fewer Recruiters than before, but many of those who left never returned. The reason for this is simple: we didn't need as many as before. Why? Among many other things, it's because HR Generalists became much more sophisticated about Talent Acquisition.

After the economic downturn began, HR Generalists were forced to pick up the slack. They learned to be better Project Managers and more open to hiring additional resources such as outsourced providers and search firms. And as the economy continued to improve, companies didn't need as many Recruiting Specialists and those recruiting jobs that did return didn't pay as much.

What was made clear are the things Recruiters and Talent Acquisition leaders have to do to survive and prosper through a downturn and as recovery begins. While opportunities will emerge in both scenarios, being prepared for both is what will make the difference – especially when more becomes out of your control.

In a tough economy Recruiters need to develop new skills and build on the ones they already have. During the recession, as requisition volumes shrank, forward-thinking companies downsized accordingly. They asked Recruiters to expand to other functional areas and stretch themselves a bit. They also took advantage of the lull to build on their foundation by focusing on the four pillars of a corporate Talent Acquisition function: process and policy, organizational structure, and alignment to the business, technology, and metrics. They used this time to strengthen each of the four foundational pieces. Despite the initial pain of downsizing, during the recession, many companies witnessed tremendous innovation. The dismal economy made them stronger. As the economy rebounded, and even got back to significant growth in some areas, Talent Acquisition teams also emerged much stronger and better able to scale their business.

Companies and divisions with operations in Europe have seen a greater adoption of the Talent Acquisition and Talent Acquisition functions. For instance, at the beginning of the most recent economic downturn, a major consumer products company streamlined their processes and utilized technology tools globally to achieve cost savings. In addition, this same company implemented a European Talent Acquisition function, which improved service to Hiring Managers and reduced costs (in the past they primarily used agencies to recruit teams).

Upgrading of talent is important. Companies have been able to take advantage of economic downturns by cleaning their "talent house" by terminating under-performing employees. This enabled them to clear space to upgrade talent and make some strategic hiring decisions. According to some corporate leaders the biggest change during this period was the opportunity to speed up performance management and upgrade talent. Some organizations incentivized executives to see the opportunity to go after talent from the other industries (especially those hit hard by the downturn such as automotive and financial services) and make some strategic hiring decisions. These organizations continued to capitalize on the employer market by using their performance management process to free up space for upgraded talent.

Companies increased brand/talent market share. They knew the importance of continuity with key business schools and while many companies scaled back significantly, others decided to take market share. Through innovative low-cost efforts they improved their presence on university Talent Acquisition and continued to hire students into their leadership development pipeline with the confidence that they will absorb them into their business. Maintaining this continuity often took some convincing on the part of executive Talent Acquisition. This strategy will pay off in droves as the economy grows. Universities and students remember companies that were their fair-weather friends and those that stayed through the downturn will benefit.

Focusing on Talent Acquisition and employee morale is always key. Companies needed to determine a different way to recognize and motivate people. Budgets were cut, and they weren't able to do the things that were always available previously. Recruiters took a very personal approach to help the team feel a sense of community. Recruiters are very social, and this is important to them.

Finally, a key point—during an economic downturn the single most consistent reason for the demise of a corporate Talent Acquisition function was that the Talent Acquisition leader did not create an optimal environment for Recruiters to be successful. No solution is better than a great in-house Recruiter. The caveat is that as a Talent Acquisition leader you must be able to identify the great Recruiters, train them effectively, and hold them accountable. This is what a great Recruiter wants.

In a recovery we know there won't be a big hiring bump but rather incremental job growth. There are many things that can be done during this time to prepare for sustained growth. Some of these things we'll explore next, like:

STREAMLINING PROCESSES

Companies can become more efficient, streamline their processes, and get their "house in order." For instance, during the recent economic downturn many organizations were so sensitive to adding any new costs that they created systems of "over-approving" offers and hires. This not only seriously impacted the cost of hiring (ironically) but created inefficient systems. A year later, these processes needed to be streamlined. More accountability can be put in the hands of Hiring Managers and, as a result, the process becomes more effective, is less costly, uses less Talent Acquisition resources, and makes greater use of technology. So whether it's giving tools to Hiring Managers to help their efficiency, improving the assessment process, or setting up the interview process so that when key talent is needed the right person can be hired, much can be improved in this area.

Despite having a smaller team, many companies managed to focus on innovation, alongside the day-to-day hiring. They found cheaper and more efficient ways to recruit. Many took the money used for advertising and used it in a couple of different areas, including external awards in order to increase brand awareness, social networks such as Twitter, Facebook, YouTube, and LinkedIn, and the integration of their career sites with their social networks through interactive blogs and channels.

Upgrading Skills of HR Generalists

Necessity was the mother of invention and the smart companies continued to upgrade the recruiting and project management skills of their HR Generalists. This entailed having HR professionals continuing to be better Project Managers—actually doing some Recruiting on their own—and effectively utilizing outside resources such as external contractors, outsource providers, and third-party search firms.

Using Recruitment Process Outsourcing (RPO) More Effectively

As you know from Chapter 7, I haven't been a big fan of full outsourcing because I always felt developing an internal Talent Acquisition capability was key to an organization's success. However, I do see a strong benefit to using RPO when there is a need, especially with respect to a geographic or specific expertise requirement. A Talent Acquisition function needs to be really good at sourcing and finding the core key job areas within their company. This is different for every organization—you need to find out what the top four or five key job areas are for your organization that are most core! Outside of that, the savvy Talent Acquisition professional can likely add more value to his/her company by managing projects effectively, rather than doing everything themselves. In addition, many RPO companies are unbundling their services in unique ways. Some of these companies take on just the scheduling of candidates or the web sourcing of candidates. Spend some time and learn more about this. We spoke at length about this in Chapter 7, so I hope the theme of keeping your most strategic roles close to the company is still resonating.

In lean economic times it is vital that companies ensure they keep people who are passionate and are great at their job even if they need to reduce their Talent Acquisition function. They should also invest in training and development for people who are left behind.

The two critical things Recruiters need to focus on are *demonstrating* their value and then *delivering* on that promise. During a downturn, organizations feel as if Talent Acquisition is unnecessary because they may not be hiring as many people. But organizations have a very difficult time in trying to recruit and attract the people they want, and in tough times, good people are harder to extricate out of their current job to come work for an organization.

And it's not always only about hiring people. Clients ask for things like optimizing the Talent Acquisition function and making their HR teams more effective. Consultants are doing a lot more training and development of Recruiters and HR people. There is more investment in university and recruiting programs and a lot of action in the RPO space, including helping companies to figure out what functions, if any, to outsource, and then helping them to make a smoother transition by brokering the relationship between the RPO company and the organization.

In good times, it's just as important to keep the momentum and strategy you applied in lean economic times as you scale the business. It's very easy to celebrate extra budget, or an increase in headcount. With the right team in place, you will be in a position to grow tenfold bringing in the right resources to help you. This is where we all aspire to be, a top team who can get the core work done faster, cheaper, and better to help the business succeed.

CHANGE MANAGEMENT: INDIVIDUAL VS. ORGANIZATIONAL

The basic principles are the same for managing change for individuals, teams, and organizations.

For individuals, for example, a Recruiter may have to follow a procedure of implementing Hiring Manager intake meetings on every new search where they did not have to before. Individuals respond to change with SARAH (reminder, this is the acronym for Shock, Anger, Resistance, Acceptance, and Help).

For teams, perhaps a Talent Acquisition team will now be implementing new metrics that measure their own performance against a goal where in the past there were just anecdotal metrics.

An organization may have to drastically change its structure, reporting relationships and whole jobs (titles, functions, and reporting relationships) along with its processes and outputs.

Employees will move through the model at different rates. Managers help employees embrace the change and influence future behavior. Encourage employees to discuss their concerns and be prepared to listen. Display confidence in the company and in Leadership. It is critical that you, as leaders, help your employees through the change. All change, whether good or bad, does cause some angst. We must provide our employees opportunities to question and internalize the change and then focus the team on the business goals and objectives. The role of the leader is to help your team members understand the change, embrace it, and then focus on the future.

How Do We Know We're Effective in the Change?

Good question. We know through three activities: thinking, feeling, and doing.

Thinking

- We assess the current state. Where are we today? Why do we need to change? Who will be impacted (stakeholders)?

- We define the future state. Where do we need to go? What will success look like (metrics)? What are the obstacles?

We formulate the rationale for the change. We create a team to execute the plan and we make sure senior Leadership and key stakeholders buy in.

We are clear about our expected outcomes.

Feeling

We communicate value. We share the business case, share the plan for how success will be achieved, and ensure understanding of individual's roles and how they will be evaluated.

The goal is to gain and increase stakeholder commitment. To do this we develop solid communication plans for all key stakeholder groups and involve stakeholders early on. We consider the personal and professional impacts to key stakeholders and address them.

Doing

Change must not be merely discussed and planned but implemented. We need to ask ourselves: How are we changing the way we do our work? How are we going to know the change has been implemented? How are we measuring the change (using the metrics established)? What accountabilities are in place? And how will resources be adjusted?

Our commitment to change must be sustained. New behaviors must be recognized and reinforced, and we need an ongoing communication plan.

We need to assess organizational impacts in areas including compensation, training, the governing model, operating mechanisms, and metrics.

Here is a case study that reveals some of the key points we are considering:

CHANGE PLAN CASE STUDY: TROUBLE IN HOLLYWOOD

At a global entertainment company with thirty thousand employees, a totally decentralized business model included Talent Acquisition organizations operating independently. They were attempting to access the same talent pools with different brands and messages.

The existing culture consisted of totally independent groups with their own unique culture and brands. They were very proud of their business and competitive with disdain for anything central or "corporate."

I knew I had to help them understand the key considerations and obstacles and how employees would feel with the kind of changes we may soon be discussing. With the possibility of centralizing the model, reactions could be anywhere from uprooted, angry, and defiant to excited and engaged.

On the external side, there would be challenges to balance as well. These were things like other business strategies being launched at specific times that may change the course of business, or the needs of a specific group. Changes of this nature could impact available talent and the candidate pool.

Recruiters needed to know how employees would react to change. They were looking for a positive outcome and the maintaining of performance.

Leadership engagement included key management messages directly from top management, including non-HR leaders. Getting business-unit leaders engaged was key.

How could the company accomplish this? By helping employees through change. Engaging employees in designing the new organizational structure, positions, and their roles. Giving them options and providing them with information about the options. Making them feel involved.

The destination and goal were not changeable. How to get there was.

Enabling the Change

What was the impact to the organization? Change in leadership and new reporting structures caused the most issues.

How did the company manage success? Baseline metrics were undertaken and goals were set *with* the team, not *for* the team. The team then managed metrics against their own goals. Overall goals of improving cost, speed, quality, and constituent satisfaction were always primary.

Having consistent dialogue with the team on issues and problems caused less team distress. There were lots of meetings and surveys. External facilitators were used. The company controlled non-planned terminations.

What Lessons Were Learned?

The process produced a lot of useful information.

Overpromises to the organization can be deadly as can underestimating the time it takes to communicate and react to team feedback. Not being willing to make hard decisions on change-resistant team members and not having external facilitation at the outset was a problem.

Guidelines for Leading People through Change:

- Prepare for the change before it occurs.

- Provide a clear description of the change and a picture of success.

- Find and remove obstacles before the change occurs.

- Allow adequate time for people to accept the change.

- Involve affected people in planning the change.

- Provide motivation for people to embrace the change.

- Find and utilize resources and people that support the change.

- Allow the change to be shaped by ongoing feedback.

- Provide clear implementation objectives for all people involved in the change.

- Continually monitor the change and adjust resource levels.

- Reinforce the new behaviors through formal and informal methods.

- View leading others through change as an ongoing process.

In summary, when entering a period of change Talent Acquisition leaders must first assess the need. Business leaders must drive the change and develop a detailed plan that begins pre-change and carries through to post-change. The effectiveness of the change must be measured.

CONCLUSION

As a consultative Talent Acquisition leader, you might think that change is the essence of our profession. After all, that's what we do—we facilitate the change of one person to another in an organizational position or we assist when a new position is created.

Within a large organization these are individual changes. We also need to know how to manage organizational changes: the global or seismic shifts in corporate culture brought about by a merger, downsizing, a new business venture, or in response to market changes. Organizational changes involve many employees—entire departments or companies. Like individual changes, but on a bigger scale, organizational changes impact employees on several levels: thinking (understanding the mechanics of change), feeling (being unafraid of change), and doing (effecting change). It is the task of the consultative Talent Acquisition leader to understand these forces and harness the power of change.

CHAPTER 11: BUSINESS IS GLOBAL – RECRUITING IS LOCAL

The lure of globalization is powerful. Managers believe that if they can sell the same widget in Denver as they sell in Tokyo, they can scale up and multiply their profits. If they can consolidate customer service operations into one call center in Mumbai, costs will be cut and revenues increased. If they can put the same tires on a car made in Brazil as on one made in Cairo, there is one less regional variation to worry about. It's all about efficiency and scale.

Across the country, MBA-anointed managers in the conference rooms and offices of top US and multinational firms say to each other, "Our widgets are sold all over the world! Now we need to globalize our Talent Acquisition efforts!"

They appoint a global head honcho of Talent Acquisition to sit in an office somewhere in the US and direct the Talent Acquisition efforts in Asia, Europe, Africa and the Middle East.

Inevitably the managers discover that people are not widgets. The CEO wonders why overseas operations seem stuck in low gear. Profits decline. Stockholders hit the "sell" button. Someone eventually gets fired.

What about globalizing recruiting? While the subjects of recruiting in Europe and Asia alone could easily fill two books, I'll offer this cautionary tale of my own experience as the US-based head of global Talent Acquisition for a worldwide media company. The story happened at a time in history and in my life when the world truly seemed to be getting smaller: communication was fast and international travel was cheap. A manager in the US could conceivably oversee an operation 5,000 miles away. But while geographical borders were disappearing, this did not mean that cultural differences were going away.

I learned that all of the strategizing, planning, and developing programs to handle recruiting around the world often miss one important mark: although business is global, effective recruiting must always be local. The following are some starting thoughts on global recruiting that apply through most regions. I'll go deeper into each region further into the chapter, and thought, if you can use these as a starting point, you will find opportunities in your own team to improve Talent Acquisition activities globally (and they can also be applied to an organization's recruiting activities overall):

Tailor to Each Culture/Country

As has been mentioned, recruiting cultures and what's accepted as recruiting norms vary from country to country and region to region. There is no "one size fits all." Thus, understand what makes the recruiting culture unique in each country or region that you work and customize your approach to address those needs.

Tailor to Each Candidate Pool

Because various countries leverage the web and technology in different ways – and some still not at all – tailoring your specific message to candidate pools helps get the word to them irrespective of whether or not they have access to the web. Since not all countries leverage the web as much as other parts of the world for recruiting, this will enable you to achieve a greater consistency in your recruiting.

Tailor Your Technology to Each Culture/Country

Remember each country or region may have its own unique tools to identify where the candidates you seek are lurking. Thus it's important to know some of the specific gathering places. Some include typical social networking and media networks, but others include other unique applications, such as Xing for example, which is much more widely used in German speaking countries than LinkedIn for professional social networking. For professional social networking this is the global standard. Exception is servers – in German and French speaking countries there are two professional copycats as well as in China. In China it's called Ushi.cn, with other popular sites Wealink.com and Tianji.com being merged into a France-based tool called Viadeo. While this company operates globally, their main focus is on France and China.

LinkedIn, while very popular in many areas, is banned or highly regulated in some countries through privacy laws or government control. While most large global players continue to use it outside of the laws using VPN to get around it, there are areas like Japan and Korea where it is not culturally accepted to openly look for a role on a social network, and areas without reliable high speed internet who do not use the tool at all.

There are tried and true tips that apply to all organizations around the world, but especially in Europe:

Train your Hiring Managers. During the past decade, management development has not had a lot of focus in many businesses and even some of the best managers need training in effective recruitment. Some Hiring Managers need significant coaching and guidance; to get the desired end result they need to give the right brief to Recruiters. It may seem obvious to you, but it's not to others. This is especially key in European environments.

Employee referrals can also take a back seat during times of economic downturn, and as things rebound, so does a candidate's willingness to make a move. It's important to continue to actively promote ERs and ensure that they have a positive image and reputation that is marketed well internationally and companywide. They are a relatively rare example of a sourcing methodology that typically works well across the whole of Europe, but be wary of these in some areas of Asia, for example, Japan. In Japan, there are cultural issues around loyalty for mid-career people, so these programs not as popular. In India and China, there is often an expectation of candidates being offered bonuses for payment, so programs require a lot of governance as they are open to a lot of mismanagement – and high risk in these countries.

Job descriptions have changed significantly in recent years. Good ones now are far more useful, and they really do describe the job instead of simply following a formularized template that Hiring Managers see as needed to "keep HR happy." The right key words and searchable terms are vital to attract the type of people with the required skills and experience. Time has been invested to ask the people excelling in their current roles how they describe what they do to help attract the succession plan, or grow the team as talent develops within the organization.

TECHNOLOGICAL AND CULTURAL CHANGES

So what has happened since then? Many things, but in a word: technology. The technological breakthroughs and developments we've seen around the world have had the greatest impact on how recruiting has evolved. That's not to say that's the only change that has occurred. Two others—the increase in globalized, multinational companies (and their need to be competitive) and the political changes, for example, the formation of the current European Union—have had an effect. But none has been as dramatic as the developments of technology and the ubiquitous nature of our access to information through the click of a mouse.

To appreciate this, it's important to see how things have evolved over time. In the twenty-first century the rate of change has increased. As much has changed in the past 10 years as in the overall 20 years prior to that. In the mid-to-late 1990s, the first Recruiting Human Resource Information Systems (HRIS) came into play with the advent of Resumix and Resutrack in the US and Bond adapt, Mr. Ted, and iGrasp in Europe. As a result, automated candidate and talent pools started to emerge, which meant that Recruiters didn't have to start from scratch with every new recruitment campaign. In addition, they could see what was available to them in the database in terms of suitable candidates and profiles. The rise of internet job boards like Monster and StepStone also had a big impact. Over the past 10 years we've seen the majority of people now willing to apply for even relatively senior roles through the web via corporate career sites as well as job boards.

Since the development of the internet it has become much easier for corporations to source candidates themselves instead of turning to agencies. It's created a paradox. On the one hand, with the variety of channels available (job boards, social networking sites, trade publications), you can source in a much more targeted way; however, this array of options also requires you to think through the sourcing plan to make sure it's the most appropriate and efficient one for each specific vacancy.

Technology has helped speed up the Talent Acquisition process in the past ten years in many parts of many regions. Whereas before candidates and agencies faxed CVs, today they e-mail or submit them through postings. This more efficient process has led to greater expectations on the part of both candidates and managers in terms of speed of response and hiring.

The development of technology (as well as the desire to lower costs) has empowered companies to develop internal Talent Acquisition mechanisms and in-house expertise. Indeed, a large part of the job transition process is still controlled by third-party agencies such as search firms and employment agencies. But the increase in the use and adoption of technological tools by both candidates and companies has increased the variety of Talent Acquisition options available to everyone involved. In effect, this has been a boon to both client and vendor.

While the world has changed enormously for agency Recruiters, because search is used far more widely than ever before, many more companies have built up increasingly sophisticated Talent Acquisition teams and capabilities in-house. Generally, we've seen a greater adoption of direct and web-based recruiting techniques and approaches in the north and less so as we move south. For instance, Scandinavian companies in Norway, Sweden, and Denmark were amongst the first to really leverage the internet for recruiting. And even today recruiting in France, Italy, and the rest of southern Europe is still not as web-enabled. However, that must be balanced for a Recruiter working in the Asia-Pacific region because in Japan, even cold calling a candidate may be a serious legal violation, and in parts of Myanmar, the use of smartphones outside the capital city is scarce.

In Eastern Europe, where they're not as concerned with the old norms of using third-party agencies, we've seen a faster adoption of internal recruiting mechanisms such as direct sourcing and the use of technology. While in Singapore and Australia, in-house Recruiters can more easily work as one team supporting regional Talent Acquisition needs in their countries. I would suggest that the idea of a much more solidly web-enabled recruitment process, where both employers and prospective candidates at all levels leverage web-based tools to find and fill jobs. But it's important to note that there are several factors that contribute to this, like cultural norms and local laws.

THE RISE OF MULTINATIONAL CORPORATIONS

While technology has undoubtedly had the greatest impact on the growth and development of recruiting globally, the rise and spread of global, multinational companies and their competitive needs has also played a significant role.

Perhaps the most important factor in this development is cost. As multinational companies grow, their need to recruit talent more efficiently and in a cost-efficient manner increases. This in turn has been a primary driver of the development of in-house recruiting departments and specialties that are distinct from general HR. This development was relatively new to even the most sophisticated recruiting departments 10 years ago, so it's still new to many companies and countries in Europe to this day. To that end, some large, but mostly medium and small, companies still do not have in-house recruiting departments. But multinational companies have a need to get the best talent faster and in a less costly manner; and, as a result, it's more efficient to recruit themselves when they can.

This is another example of how two developments can become linked and feed off of one another. In this instance, as technology has enabled in-house recruiting capabilities to flourish, and in turn, as multinational companies have spread, their desire for in-house recruiting has increased. So each feeds off the other.

The increased focus on costs associated with recruitment has also led companies to a greater awareness of the importance of internal mobility. For existing employees, internal job boards make the whole process of applying for internal roles far easier and simpler. This helps an organization make the most of its resources by retaining scarce skills whenever possible and helping to minimize the risk that is often associated with hiring people from the outside.

In addition, companies have seen the wisdom and value of buybacks— adjusting the compensation of an employee, where possible, who is a potential leaver rather than having to replace them outright.

Thus, while technology and the rise of multinationals have had the two biggest impacts on recruiting in recent memory, any discussion about recruiting would be incomplete without addressing the importance of local government and political affairs. Of course, I won't get deep into politics, but the politics of recruiting leaves much to explore.

While recruiting is best done by region, sourcing teams that work by channel will be the most successful. Allow sourcing teams to become subject matter experts in multiple regions so they can build a strategy and identify the competitive landscape. Address each channel separately, one at a time, until you identify how best to reach and communicate with local talent.

Forge strong relationships with local gatekeepers like professors, association leaders, diplomatic corps, and chambers of commerce. Ask them questions like:

- What are the top schools?

- Are they private or public?

- What is their selection process when admitting students?

- What percentage of applicants get selected? What are the top employers in the area?

- What associations or conferences are in the area?

Find your company's local HR representative, or if there is none, the equivalent of a local labor department, and ask about rules regarding what information can be solicited from prospects during initial phone conversations. Contact a local marketing company for assistance in sending out initial contact e-mails to local talent. Instead of direct recruiting, try the much safer alternative: making an introduction. And if cell phones are very common in your target country, consider using SMS instead of e-mail or phone calls.

INTERCULTURAL COMMUNICATION

When talking with people from other cultures, remember that they may consider direct solicitation to be rude and they are unsure how to react or respond to direct approaches. Recruiting by phone is less effective in countries where face-to-face meetings are highly favored. While internet use is increasing worldwide, blogging and online living are not increasing at the same rate.

Before formulating a strategy, study the cultural nuances of each target country. Take time to allow for cross-regional training or education so that teams can become subject matter experts outside of their usual region. When working across multiple regions, they will be better equipped to build a strategy, build relationships with Hiring Managers, and identify the competitive landscape.

Culturally Sensitive Issues

Here are a few of the issues facing a Recruiter from one country recruiting a candidate from another. What follows is not comprehensive and conditions are always changing. The message is that you need to use Recruiters and recruiting methods that are attractive to the population from which you need to recruit. One needless mistake can turn off a candidate who may have been perfect for the role. I'll share a few examples from various regions to give you a sense of the nuances that can get you into trouble.

Brazil – be cautious when providing feedback after interviews – even if you are asked to. If you inadvertently insult an individual, with large family networks, your brand can easily be tarnished.

Mexico – build up local networks and your overall referral program. Use these connections to gently approach prospects and allow them to feel it was your idea that you begin a dialogue.

South America – US-based Recruiters: do not be offended if you are called a "gringo." South Americans use this term to refer to people from the United States, and it is not meant to be insulting. Don't expect executive-level candidates to be on CV/resume databases or social networks; it may be seen as a sign of them looking for a job, which is a no-no.

Latin America – face-to-face meetings are highly preferred. Introductions and referrals work best. E-mail tends to be less casual but is viewed as official business.

Canada – work with your marketing team to ensure diversity language is a focus and part of every company profile.

Germany – online searches in German yield much better results. Direct recruiting tends to be viewed negatively. E-mail response is relatively high. Germans are comfortable with direct personal questions during phone interviews.

Netherlands and Denmark – Recruiters from outside this region need to make sure they probe firmly for package details of Dutch candidates who will typically tell you what they expect to earn, not what they currently earn. Part of the deal negotiation with Danish candidates can be how many newspapers and magazine subscriptions the company will pay for—much to the incredulity of the UK and US Recruiters!

France – the French do not tell or like to hear American-style jokes with punch lines. They prefer intelligent and satirical wit. Funny stories of real life situations are appreciated.

Greece – expect Greeks to ask personal questions such as "Are you married?" or "Do you have children?" This is not considered rude but rather an attempt to get to know you personally.

Russia, Romania, and Ukraine – little response to e-mail, particularly at work. Easy to find prospects on the Internet, but they become suspicious that you know so much about them even though you got it all online. Never refer to a Russian as "comrade."

Australia – Australians respect people with strong opinions, even if they don't agree, so state your point directly. Direct phone calls work best. Prospects are very approachable but are used to working through agencies.

India – when an Indian answers, "I will try," he or she generally means "no." This is considered a polite "no."

Japan – do not expect a Japanese person to say "no." "Maybe" generally means "no."

China – Chinese also find "no" difficult to say. They may say "maybe" or "we'll see" in order to save face. Some online info is in English but there's a significant amount that is not. Cultural understanding is critical in gaining their trust. Chinese people deliberate and take time to make a decision. They also prefer to have the last word in a conversation or meeting. Rank is valued and arranging meetings with business leaders goes a long way.

Vietnam – refer to Ho Chi Minh City as Saigon. Local people prefer Saigon to Ho Chi Minh City, a name imposed by the government in Hanoi.

South Africa – direct e-mail response rate is low. Prospects respond better after introductions from gatekeepers.

United States – Americans often share things in casual conversation, even with strangers, which may seem shockingly private.

Searching Online

The internet is a powerful international recruiting tool, but you have to know how to use it. The searches and search terms that work in the United States may not work in other countries. Use appropriate regional terminology. Just because you call it a resume doesn't mean Germans or Saudis do too.

"Resume" in Various Languages

When using your regular resume searches it is recommended that you replace the word "resume" for its native equivalent. Here are a few examples:

COUNTRY	TERM
United States	Resume
German	Lebenslauf
Dutch (Holland)	Samenvatting
French	Résumé
Portuguese	Resumo
Arabic	سيرة ذاتية, خِصَّة
Arabic (alt)	سيرة ذاتية, خِصَّة
Polish	Zyciorys
Swedish	Återuppta
Russian (Borat's)	Đåçþìå
Russian	*Резюме*
Spanish	Resumen
Spanish (EU)	Currículo
Greek	επαναλάβετε
Japanese	概要
Chinese	回复
Korean	이력서

Ask a local to send you the correct characters.

Translate Pages

So you found a page but can't read it? Try just clicking "Translate this page." if you have the Google Toolbar, you can right-click and select "page info" then choose "Translate into English."

Or copy the URL, go to babelfish.yahoo.com, paste it under "Translate a web page," and choose your language.

Don't know what language it is? Copy a paragraph and paste it in Fagan Finder (faganfinder.com/translate) then click "identify Language." Other translators include Free Translation (freetranslation.com) and World Lingo (worldlingo.com).

WHEN IN ROME, RECRUIT LIKE THE ROMANS DO

One of the hardest flights I ever took was from Los Angeles to London

Heathrow. It was one of those quick turnaround trips where I flew nine or ten hours for a morning meeting and then turned around and came right back.

I'm not a fan of those trips, but what made it particularly difficult was I was traveling to admit failure and all I kept asking myself was, "how did I let things get this far?"

I was scheduled to meet with the General Manager of our UK-based European music division. It was not going to be a fun meeting.

It all started because the division had needed a new head of HR. For several months prior to my trip, despite the UK division's pleas to follow some of the local recruiting protocol, I, as head of Talent Acquisition sitting in Los Angeles, insisted they do things our way. I thought I knew better.

Since they didn't have an in-house Recruiting department, the UK managers recommended we rely on an outside, third-party agency. "Nonsense," I responded. "We have more than capable Recruiters in the United States; let's handle it for you, our way."

"Let's at least pay an outside agency to place an ad to generate CVs," they suggested.

"Why would I do that," I replied, "when we can identify potential candidates and just call them directly ourselves?"

They were appalled. "You can't do that," the Brits explained. "We don't call people and directly recruit or source from other companies."

And back and forth it went. What's worse, even though there was an eight-hour time difference between us, I did not have the courtesy to set up conference calls on *their* time. Since I was sitting in the headquarters in the United States, I always got my way and threw up many hoops for them to jump through.

But we weren't getting the UK talent we needed. When I landed at Heathrow after several months of failure doing it my way and operating from the common American perspective that the world revolves around us, I wished the drop in my stomach were as soft as the thump of our wheels touching the ground. It wasn't.

I learned my lesson. As a global corporate Talent Acquisition leader, and now as the head of a management consulting firm that works with organizations all over the world, I've had a lot more experience with global business, and local recruiting. It's reinforced what I learned during that experience many years ago. In Europe there are significant cultural, legal, and regulatory differences from how Talent Acquisition is done in the rest of the world and the only way to be effective is to be sensitive to them on a country-by-country basis.

To be sure, there are values, philosophy, and some processes that can be shared across an organization globally. But to be an effective head of Talent Acquisition for an international entity, and to service internal clients in diverse regions around the world, you have to be sensitive to the differences and similarities in different regions and countries. You can think globally, but you must recruit locally, and that has never been truer than in Europe.

So if I'm a head of Talent Acquisition and I have significant operations in Europe, what do I need to know to be effective in today's fast-changing European recruiting climate?

To begin, the most fundamental mistake that many make is assuming that all countries in Europe are similar to each other. Thinking that Italy is similar to France simply because it's close by and they're both in Europe is like thinking the United States is similar to Mexico because they're both part of the Americas. It's best not to think of Europe as a single entity.

Secondly, the good news is there's a lot of change happening right now in Europe that is mirroring some of the changes that occurred in Talent Acquisition in some of the most sophisticated corporate staffing environments. But to understand that we need some historical context for how recruiting has evolved in Europe.

HISTORICAL BACKGROUND OF EUROPEAN CORPORATE RECRUITING

Though any generalization made about all of Europe is bound to be oversimplified and disrespectful, in the past there were some customs and approaches that seemed to be shared by many countries in Western Europe and the European Union.

For starters, the idea of a recruitment function as part of HR is still, to this day, relatively new to many companies. Because the HR Generalist was placed in charge of all things HR even though they didn't always have specific recruiting expertise, Hiring Managers would often look to outside, third-party agencies for their needs. In addition, before the spread of technology many companies and job seekers alike had developed established patterns of connections. Recruitment was often done through networking and referrals. The referrals were generally limited to the contacts of people at the company and tended to be limited to the "old boys" network. You even had to write a *hand-written* motivation letter and send it, together with your CV, to the personnel manager.

Because companies had HR managers who were responsible for all of HR, including recruiting, they would only start to look for candidates when there was a "burning platform." Thus there was very limited proactive recruiting or candidate generation for the talent pipeline. Due to time pressures, outside agencies were often asked to perform recruiting, which is a costly model.

A cultural holdover that dates back to the 1960s is the use of storefront

("High Street") employment agencies especially for lower-middle to entry-level roles. These are employment offices that display job openings *in their windows*. These agencies originated back when the unemployment rate was so low that companies had to physically go to the street to entice walk-in workers. These agencies are still used today for entry-level and technical jobs. Moreover, throughout many parts of Europe, candidates were generated primarily though placing advertisements in newspapers, a process called advertised selection. Back in the 1990s companies used a large number of "selection agencies." These companies required their clients—the hiring companies—to pay for large employment advertisements in major print publications in Europe. The selection agency would then screen all of the CVs that were received. You paid a high fee for this service—often 25%, not far off what a regular retained search would cost. The reason that companies used these services was primarily cultural; it was still rare for organizations to actually have dedicated internal Recruiters. In addition, they did not have the tools and resources to read and screen all of those CVs.

Recruiters were highly dependent on certain key print media titles, such as the *Sunday Times* and *Financial Times* in the UK and *Suddeutsche Zeitung* and Frankfurter *Allgemeine Zeitung* in Germany. Unfortunately, this approach was generally not considered to be good value for the money given the high advertising rates and few discounts these publications would afford. A large part of the job transition process in the past was controlled by third-party agencies, which companies relied upon to varying degrees across a highly diverse European recruiting space.

Politics and Pan-European Recruitment
The formation of the European Union (EU) undoubtedly made it easier for multinationals to spread across Europe and cross borders. Similarly, the barriers for the citizens of the EU states to work in different countries have gradually been lowered. As has been noted, though in theory the barriers to working across much of the European Union were removed in 1992 it's only been in the last 10 years that many more people, other than recent university graduates and very senior executives, have been prepared to uproot themselves to live and work in another European country. Prior to that, other than the Irish, Dutch, and a few others, it was uncommon to see European nationals in the labor market outside of their home country. There could be changes like UK exit from the European Union, or migration law changes that Talent Acquisition leaders now have to be ready for.

CHALLENGES OF STAFFING IN THE NEW EUROPE

The idea and practical realities of pan-European recruiting and a pan-European Talent Acquisition function are at best conflicted and complex. The biggest mistake anyone can make when it comes to considering recruiting throughout Europe is to consider Europe one place and not a collection of independent, individual countries that happen to be located next to one another. It's important that non-Europeans understand the strong sense of nationalism throughout the region and that a fatal approach would be to consider it "the United States of Europe." It's the truth behind this sentiment that makes pan-European Talent Acquisition so challenging.

Another challenge to successfully running a pan-European recruiting function lies in managing an array of Recruiters across a diverse geographical and cultural landscape. While there are some tools, philosophy, and selection methods that can be shared across a company, it is challenging to require a Recruiter in one country to move too closely to the style and approach of a Recruiter (or boss!) in a different country, and it's asking for trouble. The ideal scenario is to have local Recruiters who are capable of, and committed to, recruiting to the internationally agreed-upon company standards and who use the companywide adopted software tools and selection methods.

Anyone who has recruited in Europe for any length of time will have learned very rapidly that local knowledge and capability is vital and that the approach to the recruitment challenge varies enormously from country to country. To this end, there are cultural, legal, and language issues that make any notion of easily recruiting an individual from one country to another remote at best. Even if one country is a half hour's drive from another, the metaphorical recruiting "fences" along the borders can be tall.

What might work in one country, such as calling or sourcing directly, may be considered crass or unacceptable for its next-door neighbor. Additionally, language differences cannot be overlooked.

There also are differences in laws and regulatory compliance from one country to the next. Even within countries there are local laws related to work councils and unions that complement national labor negotiations.

Recruitment is still a highly localized activity with many pitfalls for the unwary Recruiter from abroad. However, companies can and do have successful pan-European recruitment activities as long as they adopt an approach that balances a corporate philosophy, strategy, and technology with specific local needs.

Having a pan-EU function makes sense in terms of expertise development, system use, and overall Talent Acquisition strategy. However, to be able to present high-quality, finalist candidates, you will always need local Recruiters on the ground when you are Talent Acquisition at operational levels. With executive levels, having a central EU or even global function may work quite well. On the lower levels, because of language constraints, candidate proximity, lack of knowledge and understanding of the local labor market and sourcing trends, and understanding of the business needs, Recruiters should stay local.

Overall, the best approach is to keep organization, strategy, and system development *central* and operational Talent Acquisition activities and candidate/business contacts *local*. The ideal scenario is to have expert local Recruiters who are capable of and committed to adopting the internationally agreed company standards and who use the company-wide software tools and selection methods.

Key Tips and Tools for Talent Acquisition in Europe

A StepStone Solutions talent report, written in cooperation with the Economist Intelligence Unit, indicated that after the global recession, the rebounding economy offered renewed optimism about prospects for economic growth. Although a recovery was welcome, it is always the start, not the end, of a new journey. A post-recessionary environment will see companies at a crossroads where critical decisions on managing talent will need to be made. The message from the survey of global executives is that businesses must concentrate on people and on their business talent—and do so urgently.

Successful Talent Acquisition teams in Europe have never been more vital to a global company. Thus, given where things were and how far they've come in Europe, what are some tips, tools, and techniques that will enable Talent Acquisition leaders to manage recruiting across Europe most effectively?

To begin, some basic, fundamental relationship building is critical. It's been noted by experts in the field that traveling to the region and having some personal face time is important (ideally, unlike my early experience, before you hit bumps in the road). Demonstrate your desire to listen to colleagues in the region and understand their business and talent needs in person. It's strongly recommended it not be done over the phone or in an e-mail.

Secondly, considering each country in Europe on its own terms (and recruiting locally) is not only an important mindset and approach—it extends to systems and processes. It's important to not assume that systems and processes designed for one particular region will work in Europe (or even ones designed for one country in Europe will automatically work for another in the area). Be prepared to adapt them, at least to a degree, to allow for local differences.

It's also recommended that application processes generally be kept simple with as few clicks as possible. Candidates are used to using simple and well-designed websites for e-commerce purposes. They will not have the patience to follow an outdated web-based job application process. A company has to have a high-quality careers section of their corporate site or even a microsite. Applicants—whether direct or via other sources—will review the careers pages and Recruiters can save a lot of valuable interview time if many of the typical FAQs have already been answered via the careers pages.

In the coming years, job boards will evolve quickly. Many candidates now skip job boards initially and go straight to search engines like Google to search for their desired role. Search Engine Optimization (SEO) is therefore increasingly important.

For example, StepStone had a position for a temporary Berlin-based English-speaking paralegal. A German national based in the UK who was looking to return to Germany for a few months searched through Google for the role she was looking for, was taken to the StepStone posting for the job, and successfully applied. Her route to the job posting was undoubtedly different to the one she would have made just a couple of years earlier.

However, it's noted that even with improved technology and access, there are still challenges. Undoubtedly the web has made the process of finding candidates far easier where the required skills are ubiquitous and work permits are available; the challenge, however, is that companies can now expect to receive job applications from literally all around the world, and there is the real risk that potentially hundreds of people may apply for certain roles where either the employer does not need to bring in talent from abroad or where the odds of receiving a work permit are minimal.

Social media is also a vital tool these days (although outside the US there is little evidence yet that it has been used very successfully for direct sourcing). It's been noted that LinkedIn is now very powerful, as is Xing in Germany, Austria, and Switzerland, and Viadeo in France. Many companies are still not making the right use of social media and many fail to appreciate how effective a candidate's personal marketing page can be on the web.

While we're on the subject of the web, European privacy laws that protect people can also be a big factor in your success. Think about your ATS – it has a lot of information stored within it and a privacy policy that likely follows where your headquarters is operated from. If you have a global ATS and are storing data outside of the EU, and the server is in the US, there are privacy laws against this. Be sure not to get caught in this violation as it can be significant and impact your employer brand among other things. It is prohibited to store EU privacy data in a database that is not physically located in the EU. Russia is another country where privacy laws are heavily enforced and important to know. A pharmaceutical company I once worked with was using a global ATS and ran into issues because the ATS service provider was not certified in Russia. This meant they had no local server, and in turn, was not legal to use locally, where my client was trying to grow their business. There has also been talk over the years about Russia banning the use of LinkedIn if a local database is not moved into their country.

While recruiting in Europe has changed significantly over the past several years, there are still complexities that are unique to its composition of so many developed countries occupying such a small space. Many of those challenges and cross-border barriers will remain until other changes (political and otherwise) occur. But while in the past recruitment in many countries and companies in Europe may have appeared to outsiders to be less advanced than in other regions of the world, things are changing fast! As technology continues to evolve and become ubiquitous, as multinationals continue to grow and seek efficiencies and cost decreases, and as neighboring countries in Europe continue to lower the barriers to working together, the whole of Europe, including its many individual countries and companies, will indeed be on the cutting edge of the recruiting universe.

WHAT HAPPENS IN RIO, CAN BE A LESSON FOR LIMA

As a global consultative Recruiter, you need to develop and maintain a separate strategy for each region, taking into consideration local customs and idiosyncrasies. We just talked about Europe, and now I'd like to move south to share some success practices and experience on Latin America. This area continues to grow and with its emerging middle class, it's a hotbed for global growth and talent. While Brazil is a little different because its national language is Portuguese, not Spanish like the majority of countries in the region, there is a distinct recruiting culture (more on Brazil soon!).

Loyalty is highly valued in Latin American Talent Acquisition. It has shaped the way we approach candidates, and made attracting more senior candidates that much more difficult. Discretion is the key word when working within loyalty cultures, for example, many were slow to join LinkedIn because the perception that you were looking for a new job was highly stigmatized. While that has slowly turned around, the creed still seems to follow that the more senior you are, the more discreet you need to be. It's not uncommon for interviews to take place in bars, cafés and restaurant instead of in the office because a candidate can be fired if they are seen at a competitor interviewing.

REGIONAL FLUIDITY IN LATIN AMERICA

Once you're past the discreet interviews, a large consideration for candidates in Latin America is a unique geography in that it's a large space, with multiple countries all speaking the same language. There is a lot of mobility between countries, even more than Europe and Asia because of culture and language.

From Chile to Peru, Ecuador to Argentina, these markets tend to be more fluid, especially in higher paying jobs. Pan-Latin American recruiting in Spanish speaking countries makes for easier sharing of resources without language barriers. It is not uncommon for large companies to have a large team that recruits across the region and have shared resources to cover large multi-country areas, it is much more fluid than most places in the world.

You can find many benefits in a regionalized Latin American Talent Acquisition function because you don't need a team in each country. Your back office functions can co-locate, and having a local presence for lower level jobs allows for the personal relationships to be built which are essential to building trust.

It is also not uncommon for the Latin American Talent Acquisition Team to be located in a headquarter office that is located in the United States, or more specifically, Miami, Florida. While this long-term practice is becoming more expensive to operate, there have been more operations offices moving into South America in recent years.

BRAZIL AND HER UNIQUENESS

While many Brazilians speak Spanish in addition to their native tongue, Portuguese, the country has many large cities to choose to work from. This means mobility within the country is often a first choice over relocating elsewhere in Latin America, or the world. Culturally, you will often see the same warm, friendly culture coming through, with a similar focus on keeping job searches discreet.

Where things stand out a little more for Brazilians is the wish list within their roles. It's not just compensation based – in this country's largest cities, traffic can be quite daunting. Office locations with parking is a common 'must have' request by top talent if they drive, or proximity to transit. After long commutes, Brazilians are often concerned about working hours and flexibility. They go hand-in-hand really, after a long commute, people do not want to be in cultures where they also have to physically be in one place for long hours and imprisoned by the office walls no matter what. This is an important recruiting device in understanding how to achieve a competitive edge over other employers.

REGIONAL LURES AND DETRACTORS

Like everywhere in the world, Latin America has many advantages as a place to do business, and there are also some pitfalls. I always like to tackle challenges first, so let's start with unions.

Unions are a way of life in many parts of the world. They are often established to protect workers, and enforce certain standards that were felt employers did not uphold. As global safety standards and employee experience have become strong focus areas at most companies, some of the union function has become obsolete, however, they are omnipresent in Latin America. You can expect many lower level workers to be represented by the union and it will be important to form the strongest partnership that you can with the union leaders.

To counter the challenges of working with unions, a strong attract strategy countries in the region use is tax shelters. There are a number of tax-free zones where countries can set aside places for international companies to operate tax-free. This applies in several Caribbean countries as well. Some of countries that offer this include Nicaragua, and the Dominican Republic, where you can find large office parks that all qualify for the tax-free benefits.

Not only does the tax benefit apply to the company, but employees as well. Your employees in these offices will pay a lot less income tax and have secure employment under a management contract of operations. You can imagine this is a very attractive compensation package, especially for those coming from higher taxed countries. To encourage retention of employees, many who work in a tax-free zone have non-solicitation agreements, which prohibit hiring from another company in the free-zone. This means that you can't directly apply to another employer in the nearby office park and most employers in Latin America carry some sort of policy related to this.

Overall, Talent Acquisition in Latin America has seen exciting transformation as many countries emerge into developing or developed worlds. Conditions are constantly improving in many areas which stimulates economic growth and encourages companies to capitalize on emerging markets. Another rapidly changing region is Asia-Pacific, so let's go there next.

TALENT ACQUISITION IN THE ASIA-PACIFIC REGION

I asked a respected Talent Acquisition leader who works for a successful globally-focused firm based in Singapore to tell me about the region. Adele has over 20 years' experience in HR and Talent Acquisition in the Asian region. Her role in Talent Acquisition involved starting up, designing and improving Talent Acquisition processes for organizations she has worked for. I wondered what someone leading the function from inside the region, versus from afar, like I had, would say. Diversity and complexity were the key themes she identified first when describing Asia-Pacific Talent Acquisition. "It's really a multitude of many countries in one region; no one speaks the same language, no one has the same government, or the same level of economic progress" was what she revealed. As you can see, this is quite a different challenge from Latin America and its ability to regionalize. With a vast geographic footprint in addition to the uniqueness of each country, these challenges make for an interesting mountain to climb.

When we look at China, Indian, South East Asia, we can get a lot of shared resources between these areas in many cases. While there are distinct differences, to Adele's point, there are also opportunities to look at countries with similar aspects to leverage resources, even if they are not next door neighbors. Singapore, Australia, The Philippines and Thailand are also countries that can be supported regionally as you search for the best talent. It is recommended to have local support though for bilingual aspects, and of course, relationship building.

JAPANESE TALENT ACQUISITION CHALLENGES

While many countries can be grouped in the Asia-Pacific region, Japan is an island, both literally and figuratively. In addition to a unique language, they have very specific rules and cultural practices that are followed in recruiting. A very strong work ethic and commitment to the company they work for make changing companies in Japan less likely than in other places – and they have been the same for a long time.

Japanese workers' commitment to the company – and often the first company they started working for after studying – is often both a personal value, and a cultural practice. It is seen as particularly disloyal to change a company before retirement and therefore wasn't done very often. As the tides started to change with Japanese professionals looking for more career mobility, not every company viewed their workforce as mobile. I always found this noteworthy because it further slowed Talent Acquisition professionals from approaching Japanese talent for roles outside of Japan.

If an in-house Recruiter were to reach out to someone in Japan, they would be seen very negatively. For a Hiring Manager to reach out to someone inside another company and ask if they want to quit and join your team is not done. The cultural norm is for an agency to complete this initial reach very discreetly – regardless of the level of the job. The practice of using search firms that are set up to do the work is necessary because companies cannot easily directly approach candidates. This makes the cost for Talent Acquisition quite high, but there are some good reasons for it as well. Many search firms in Japan will use their own ATS for example and in order to review or retain candidate information, a company will have to buy the search package as a whole. Candidates and search firms seem to be more comfortable with local tools instead of the centralized one you may be able to use across the rest of the region, or perhaps even globally. The focus in Japan for many has been to maintain the status quo – even as many other things change.

Some lasting relics that still work well in Japan include job ads in magazines. There are many publications that have printed ads still that candidates can review and contact an agency about. The ads are generally posted by the agency as an attract strategy that has stood the test of time to this point. After receiving some resumes, the agency will present the candidates to the companies they are providing services for.

While Japan often stands alone from a Talent Acquisition perspective, if there is an opportunity to combine efforts with one other country, it will be South Korea. While South Korea has more open recruiting, their cultural practices are the most similar to Japan and can create an opportunity to combine teams that support these two countries. While combining these efforts, know that much of it will remain very traditional, even in the medium used to connect with candidates. Traditional phone calls, formal letters, and paper-based contracts have not seen the same transformation that other countries have. There will be very little engagement through apps, texting, push technology, and other virtual connection tools in Japan and to an extent, South Korea. Another point to note is also the importance of status and hierarchy in both countries and thus a barrier for internal recruiters to approach senior candidates if they are not perceived as senior enough in their organization.

In terms of your in-house approach to Talent Acquisition, I have recommended the 80/20 rule to many of my global clients. That is, take care of the countries you can have the greatest effect on, and tread cautiously where you need to when it comes to Japan for now.

APPROACHING CANDIDATES ACROSS ASIA-PACIFIC

While Japan may not have jumped into the digital age of Talent Acquisition with both feet yet, many other counties have raced there quickly. Cultural differences have set the tone for how candidates are approached and their willingness to change jobs, and the practice of using agencies is transforming quickly.

Internet penetration rates are a key indicator that can help you identify your Talent Acquisition strategy in many parts of the region. The rate can let you know how developed an area is, be an indicator of how to source talent, and may be an indicator of the available talent in the area. Think about China for example, while they have a very aggressive recruiting style and an extremely competitive market for candidates, the proliferation of internet use is only ubiquitous within the educated populations with higher incomes. Combine this with a slow turn to allow companies to directly approach candidates through tools like LinkedIn (I say 'like' here because of the government rules around accessing "western" tools I mentioned earlier), and it can be challenging to find great talent. Outside of an online approach, the majority of lower and middle classes tend to not only have less connectivity, but the language barrier will become larger. Local language becomes much more important if you are looking to staff a plant outside a major urban center than if you are looking for analysts in highly populated city.

In The Philippines, they have a relatively good internet penetration rate versus the population as a whole. This is great for your ability to post roles, use your ATS, and even source candidates on social media. The challenge here is that there are many inconsistencies in the quality of education – so while you can access available talent online, many candidates, especially for junior level roles, may not speak English, and could even communicate in a very specific local dialect.

In India, much like China, the aggressive style of recruiting is a necessity as candidates are searching for the best opportunities. They are also highly mobile and for the right role, top talent is willing to move to similar, or even far-away parts of the world. With the large pool of technology talent in many areas of India as well, multi-national companies are setting up shop locally hoping to be a stomping ground for candidates who are not tied to the company for life and are quick to consider changing opportunities to continue growing their careers and earning potential. Many people in India are also open to being contacted by text message or a direct cold call.

As you move into South East Asia, Hong Kong, Singapore, Malaysia, Australia, and New Zealand, many of these countries have a high internet penetration and are more open to direct recruiting style. While I am not an anthropologist, we can hypothesize that these former colonized countries have a linger style from their colonizer and therefore you see a few more similarities to the European practices that span across the region.

How we approach candidates has always been part art, and part science. Understanding local and cultural practices is always a top priority for Talent Acquisition leaders – it will help your team avoid local faux pas that can hurt your ability to attract the best talent, and could even land you in legal trouble.

COMMON PRACTICES USING SEARCH FIRMS

There are many occasions when the company will not have any contact with candidates during the sourcing stage. While the full Talent Acquisition function is not often outsourced in this region, sourcing is frequently managed through agencies. It's an expensive practice and while the service provided is not always perfect, agency outreach is common and in many countries, expected.

Part of the role of the Talent Acquisition leader is to educate and help the business understand the value of their team. In the region, this has been a difficult challenge because there is a high level of distrust from candidates when Recruiters reach out to them. Part of the reason for this could be tied to regions where internet job boards are fairly new. Imagine a place like Myanmar where they are not using LinkedIn, and registration on a job board is very new to them as they become more industrialized. When you map out the market and create your sourcing strategy, if there are very few candidates on the internet, it has been left for familiar faces to let others know through word of mouth that they are hiring. Your referral networks, your internal candidates, and even the pools available to source from in companies is scarce if they do not use a well-known search firm.

Most important is perhaps advice I provide earlier in the book as it relates to using RPO and that is in the Asia-Pacific region, while it is common to work with search firms, it's important not to outsource your 'mojo'. There is a need for your team to keep strategic recruiting and all or some of the senior recruiting within your team. As teams grow and budgets are reviewed – and let's face it, often cut – the only way to continue to provide the talent the organization needs is to build capabilities internally which build relationships and save cost.

CHALLENGES TO PLAN FOR

Adele is not only an expert, she is someone who has come across significant challenges in leading her team of Talent Acquisition professionals. Not everything her team does is faster or cheaper, but they are better than trying to implement practices that do not meet the local cultural norms, or that are not legal. When I asked her what the greatest challenges she faces as the leader in the Asia-Pacific region is, "If you have learned in a more developed country, you need to put it all away." I value this advice as someone who also learned through trials and tribulations that one regions approach to Talent Acquisition is not a blanket approach for all global recruiting. The uniqueness of each market, the maturity of technology and tools, and the business needs of each market are all things that the Talent Acquisition leader needs to have awareness of.

This is a heavy task, and I'm not suggesting that you know everything about each local market – this would be impossible. What I am suggesting is that when you enter the Asia-Pacific market, make sure you follow the RecruitCONSULT! approach which is a focus on business being global, but recruiting being local.

Another significant challenge is building the internal muscle needed to own, at minimum, the strategic recruiting functions. To do this, a Talent Acquisition leader should be looking for people with core skills, and people who can grow and develop as the markets change and needs for challenge change. Recruiting talent from executive search firms is also a common practice when building your in-house teams as they complement people who are already working for the company. It has also been suggested that a new area to source talent for Talent Acquisition in Asia – Pacific countries is to hire directly from the business. If you have a fantastic salesperson who is looking for new opportunities and open to learning HR and recruiting, there may be a very valuable career growth opportunity for them under your tutelage.

While innovative and very fast to transform in some areas, overall, it's important to acknowledge that in this region, the level of sophistication that you see in Europe or North America will not be present. Talent Acquisition is a fairly new function in many areas and capabilities are still being built as functions hit the ground hard on the transactional portions of the function. Change management is an area to invest in – not only in teams that transfer to the region, but for the business. It's a big test for anyone who comes from the outside to understand the complexities, and bring assumptions that things will be similar.

MIDDLE EAST AND AFRICAN VIEWPOINTS

Bringing assumptions often comes from having a specific set of experiences. It's not that any of us want to intentionally make incorrect guesses about how things are, or should operate, but we often do through learned experiences. This is what made my recent chat with Alan, an Irish Talent Acquisition leader who is working in the United Arab Emirates (UAE), so interesting. His global experience started in the UK before he moved to Dubai and he quickly learned many lessons that he shared with me. We started our conversation talking about how relationship-driven recruiting is in the Middle East, and none of us are surprised by that. The slant on relationships that shows a very different viewpoint was the emphasis on money. "Even a few thousand dollars up front could sway a candidate to make a move" he told me.

Where money is a powerful currency in candidate movement in the Middle East especially, he also shared how difficult it was for him to initially accept (not embrace, he emphasized) that the culture is quite discriminatory. From a local viewpoint in many countries in the region and a workforce that is 90% male, it is perfectly acceptable for them to post ads looking for female candidates, from The Philippines to work in PR for example. While as a leader he had to be mindful of this approach to sourcing talent, it was also important to balance the company's global brand. It's one thing to follow local customs in a respectful way, it is another to have the local customs that are specific to a region take over your employer brand globally – even if it's the law locally. As you can see, this is yet another example of doing business globally, and recruiting locally.

RETURNING HOME – A COMMENT ABOUT EXPATS

There is a common thread when recruiting in the Middle East and African region and that is many people at the more senior levels speak English. This makes regional support much easier, as well as the opportunity for mobility of talent. That is, if there weren't very specific laws around Nationalism to consider. Let's take Saudi Arabia, Algeria, and South Africa for example. With their 'hire local' laws, it's very difficult to get top talent moved in, or out of these countries. The same applies for Turkey – and with all of these countries, the commitment to employ within means an additional lack of diversity.

Egypt is a country that has seen a lot of their talent move to other parts of the region for various reasons. Many of them have landed in Saudi Arabia and the UAE and as the social and political situation changes in Egypt, recruiting efforts are made to attract expatriates back into the country. It is not uncommon to see an influx of talent return home as more opportunities and greater safety are achieved. There was a time before LinkedIn (which is king in this region and many people rely on it to find their next role), where Recruiters struggled to find talent locally and obey these laws because candidates would indicate they were already in a country, when really, they were not. The attraction strategy to a place where there is very little tax, but rules about who could be hired meant sourcing had to ensure someone was actually in the country, or eligible to work there and this became very time consuming.

Recruiting remains almost 100% local in most of the region from the most junior roles right up to executives. Where you can leverage more of a regional or global team are the Gulf countries like Qatar, UAE and Bahrain. In the Gulf countries, you will see many expats from around the world, particularly Europe in the executive roles. Even members of your own Talent Acquisition teams may be attracted to roles in the Middle East or Africa for this reason.

ATTRACTING TALENT ACQUISITION TO THE AREA

In addition to the low income and personal tax rates employees pay, there are also many Talent Acquisition professionals who are attracted to the shift in recruiting. There has been a marked shift from using agencies for just about everything, to a direct source model. This shift, coupled with the culture that is a little less aggressive than say, North American recruiting, is very tempting. Without the same level of urgency, Recruiters working in local markets are gaining more and more traction to keep their services in-house and build capabilities there.

While women make up a small part of the workforce, there are many female Recruiter roles to play. I asked Alan if they were hampered in doing their role because of the gender inequalities that exist and was pleased to learn that women were still having great success as Recruiters in the region and that their skills were being recognized, especially in multinational and global organizations.

One of the challenges of the region is that while there has been a shift to more direct hiring, agencies are still being used often – and not in strategic ways. While it is good to have an agency to take care of the low value, high time tasks, like administration, scheduling etc., it is not good to have the in-house Recruiter hire the agency to do the sourcing and hiring. Sometimes, old habits die hard and as employers move through this change and engage employees in RecruitCONSULT! discussions about bringing high value activities from the inside of the organization, there can be slip-ups. This is an internal red flag if your team ends up pushing paper in order to support an agency who is providing the most valuable tasks to your organization.

LEADING TALENT ACQUISITION IN MANY DESERTS

Keeping your 'mojo' in the organization is important in almost every region. Engagement of the team remains a critical part of staying ahead of the competition as well. As change is continually happening, I asked Alan for his top tips for leading a high performing Talent Acquisition team in the region and here's what he shared:

1. Keep driving direct sourcing. This goes hand in hand with keeping the most valuable business at the core of your team, but also keeps your

Recruiters engaged and close to the businesses they are helping to grow.

2. Ensure consistency in processes across the region and hold people accountable. While processes may be different globally, locally, there are specific areas that can and should be streamlined. For example, the candidate experience should not vary greatly between countries.

3. Leverage referrals. Relationships and networks are especially powerful in this region and a good referred candidate is very likely to be successful. As many on your team might end up being expats, the talent pool available to you through referrals is truly vast and very global.

4. Use agencies wisely. There are some very time consuming tasks, for example background screening. This is in part because culturally, it's acceptable and common for candidates to put family, neighbors, and friends instead of former employers. Having an agency manage this for you to ensure the references are legitimate can have a significant impact on the longevity of employees – read, it's expensive to have them turn over every six months because you didn't know that was their pattern. Don't let your team get bogged down in this type of administrative rat hole.

5. Use data to change behaviors. Change management is tough, especially if you are an expat leader in a new area. What Alan was able to do in order to change perceptions of the Talent Acquisition function was done mostly with data. Disproving common misconceptions with hard evidence and arming your Recruiters with the same will help you lead your team to success.

As you lead the function in this region, you'll come across some hurdles – nothing you can't handle. Let's talk about what a few of those are next.

MANAGING VOLUME

When it comes to the work your team will do in the region, there are a few areas where volume is a concern. One cultural norm is that candidates put a lot of information on their resumes. It's not the same as in Latin American countries, where you might see a glamour shot and details about their hobbies. In many Middle East and African countries, you're getting sensitive information, like the equivalent of a social security number. As we talked about earlier, since discrimination is common, many candidates add details that would not be shared, or even be allowed to question in other parts of the world. Marital status, and number of children are common and used as decision points. For example, a married man with three children is often perceived to be more stable than a single male with no children who is the same age. Managing this volume of information – whether it's to try not to factor it into the hiring process, or to remove it before Hiring Managers can see is something to consider.

Another area where volume is an issue is unqualified candidates. Don't scoff, I know many of us have seen applicants who are grossly underqualified, or would never be considered a good fit for a role. In this region however, an open role posted to a job board could have hundreds of applicants within a few days, and the majority of the resumes are nowhere near qualified for the role. For example, a career bus driver applies for an IT Director role with no experience, education, or certifications in IT, at all.

While these may seem like small issues, they are both common across the region, and have the potential to throw you off your strategic game of delivering high quality candidates faster and cheaper than anyone else.

CONCLUSION

The goal of this chapter has been to illuminate a basic axiom of global recruiting: that while business may be global, recruiting is local. I've provided a few examples of potential pitfalls and proven solutions, but this chapter is not intended to be a comprehensive encyclopedia of international recruiting. I just wanted to give you a flavor of some of the challenges and how to overcome them.

As consultative Recruiters, we are in the business of not only finding the right person to occupy a role but to remember that the human being we recruit has dreams, aspirations, and cultural beliefs that may be deeply cherished. The Recruiter wants to be welcomed into the organization as a friend and colleague and not be made to feel as though they are suddenly working among strangers.

It's important not to globalize your Talent Acquisition function – as you can see, even from this sampling of info from across the world, each region should be approached as its own talent hub. Your global strategy has to include localization, from tools and technology, to understanding local governments, to managing agencies appropriately.

Corporate culture can make or break an enterprise. For a painful lesson, one only has to look back at the disastrous union of Daimler-Benz and Chrysler. When Daimler bought Chrysler in 1998 in what was called a merger, it wasn't long before Chrysler executives complained the stubborn Germans wouldn't listen to the Americans. The high command in Stuttgart issued orders to Detroit about everything from where the combined headquarters would be located (Germany) to what kind of business cards would be used. The Daimler execs weren't bad people; they just had a vastly different conception of what the merger meant and how to run the business. Nine years into the deal Daimler sold Chrysler at a loss. Clearly, in the Daimler-Chrysler deal, corporate culture had not been part of the discussion.

Failure to make cultural concerns part of the recruiting process leads to trouble on three levels: you may miss qualified candidates because you aren't identifying them, you may drive away qualified candidates because you offend them, and you may hire a candidate who will not fit into the existing corporate culture.

On the other hand, skillful and sensitive international recruiting can create a vibrant and rich working environment that helps an organization grow and flourish in today's increasingly complex world.

CHAPTER 12: RECRUITCONSULT! LEADERSHIP FOR OVERALL SUCCESS

Vision is not just the ability to grow the business, but understanding what it takes to package that for your customers, candidates, and clients. Talent Acquisition is not rocket science – yes, I said it! The most important skill is setting and managing expectations well with everyone you interact with. Your team needs to understand what to do when, how they are managed, and how they are evaluated. Your constituents, Hiring Managers and HR Generalist partners need to know the value you add so they can bring you in early, and so they show up when you invite them in. Once you do this, execution is more important than anything else. You must be able to deliver on your promises.

WHY POWERPOINT DOESN'T PROVE YOUR SUCCESS

At one of the first companies I worked at as the Talent Acquisition leader, I replaced someone who hadn't done a good job. I listened to the challenges the team had previously and then thought up all the ways I was going to make things better. It was brilliant and I thought I did a great job articulating it through a bunch of PowerPoint slides. I took myself on a roadshow and told people how I was going to make their lives better. I had every base covered – fewer search firms and agencies, high quality candidate sourcing, faster processes for approvals and we'd spend less money for all these great things.

This approach did not work at all. I didn't *show* them when I could do, I *told* them what I was going to do. The challenge with telling and not showing is that once you share these grand plans in all their glory, the moment it's not as great as planned, your credibility is shot for a long time. This is a difficult position to climb out of easily, or quickly for that matter. I learned a hard lesson that you don't go out telling them what you're going to do, you do it and show them. I try hard to coach and teach that now – always show, don't tell, show through execution. This way you have very tangible stories, examples, dashboards and the likes to make your trusty PowerPoint, or whichever medium you choose to share from. Showing proven success is much more credible than the sometimes abstract future and all the changes that need to happen to achieve a future state.

A RECRUITCONSULT! LEADER'S ABILITY TO INSPIRE AND MOTIVATE

In recruiting, there is a difference between high performing and inspired. High performing means that Hiring Managers, candidates, stakeholders, etc. are generally happy with the service, quality, cost, pipeline that they are receiving from your team.

Inspired is the next level. These would be people who bring a passion for the business and the people they are bringing in. They understand what levers to pull to help the business be successful, and what the future might look like, so they can find talent to meet those needs beyond today.

I won't generalize leaders as there are so many styles. What I do want to focus on is the profile of two common Talent Acquisition leaders I have encountered often. One kind can spin a fantastic story, explains all they do really well and connects with people in a real way – but they often can't fully execute and are terrible at change management. The second kind is fantastic at execution, gets the job done better, faster, and more efficiently than any others – but they but can't sell it well and don't inspire the crowds. Let me demonstrate these two types with more color, let's call them Jerry and Larry.

Jerry and Larry worked at a technology company that was booming – both as HR leaders. Jerry, the head of Talent Acquisition, was fantastic at storytelling and drawing people in to see and embrace the future. He'd host a town hall meeting, or record a video message and passionately paint a grand picture of how valuable the team was, how bright the future would be, and how by making a few changes, everyone would continue to flourish. He motivated and excited people and was commonly asked to speak to other groups as the HR darling – winning hearts and minds as he shared how his team would shape the future. Jerry's skill at this was unsurpassed. Where he had room to improve was in the execution of it all. He had a great team under him working hard to get it done, but struggled with 1:1 talent development. Where the rubber hits the road in terms of translating direct performance into meaningful dialogue was a challenge for Jerry. He had a hard time helping his team take the vision to a coaching and mentoring level.

His counterpart Larry on the other hand was leading HR strategic programs, like Business Continuity, Relocation, and Compliance – so he worked
very closely with Jerry. Larry however, was not a very good storyteller. A
member of his team once recited to me the rendition he gave of comparing
their business to repairing his own furnace at his vacation house. Now some
people would take that story and really make it memorable. This leader got too
caught up in the literal story and had many blank stares from people who both
didn't own vacation homes, and who would not bother to try and fix their own
furnace. People generally came out of Larry's meetings feeling a little deflated
and anxious to get back their tasks. Where people really flocked to Larry was
in his ability to coach 1:1 and help his team see how their role connected to
the bigger picture and the value they brought to the organization. He also was
always on the ground floor with his sleeves rolled up helping people move
initiatives forward and removing roadblocks for them.

Both Jerry and Larry were effective leaders. They both had strengths and
areas to improve – as we all do. The lesson to take away from these leaders
is that whether you soar at the 30,000 foot level, or are the best and most
granular leader, that both are required to inspire and motivate your team.

There are a few questions to ask yourself as a pulse check. It's not to say
you will change overnight and emerge a different person. Self-awareness and
the ability to understand your own development opportunities will also help
with your overall ability to lead your team to success. In no particular order,
ask yourself;

- Are you connecting? Are the conversations between you and your team
  tying the work you do to how the business will make or lose money?

- Are you acknowledging the day to day contributions? Does your team
  realize on a daily basis how they help the business succeed?

- Have you acknowledged that recruiting is very emotional for ALL
  stakeholders? Can you do this from the beginning of each hire, and
  make sure you are separating yourself if there is a possibility that your
  influence will cause a significant shift in positive or negative energy.

- Are you aware of the competition in our world? Talent Acquisition
  can be managed more effectively than other parts of HR. We can
  measure so many metrics – from pipeline, satisfaction, time, speed,
  and cost to name a few. The training team cannot be this granular,
  nor can benefits, relocation, or technology. This means there is often

a competitive spirit within HR, and also between recruiting teams. Know that this exists and it can allow really great leaders to be able to shift the strategy on communication, and leverage the competition to drive higher performance.

- Are you the only voice of leadership in your organization? Don't be – it's a lonely place to be. Bring others that are not part of your organization in to talk to your team, or on behalf of your team – internally and externally. They can share what you would have – so it's not always you. At a staff meeting, guest speakers from another business, or a team looking at metrics the same way you do to teach about process. Then you can coach your team to be part of taking on best practices, instead of letting them know their current process isn't working. This also helps as HR professionals are often skeptical of each other – an external voice can bring more credibility.

CONCLUSION

There are many great resources to help you understand leadership. There are basic principles that even land more strongly in Talent Acquisition. The most important thing you can do to prepare is be nimble to ride the wave of things going up and down. Keep focused on your end destination which is to run the best Talent Acquisition function possible and know how to share the story of function with others. If your costs go up in a quarter or two and you promised lower costs, know that sometimes you have to go back to go forward. Some quarters you may spend a lot investing in capabilities of your team. That is how you'll be able to keep the core and most strategic jobs in-house and not spend so much more on RPO. Manage how the setback helps to get to the destination and always bring your team along on that journey. The business may quickly forget all the work your team did to get top talent into the organization. It remains up to you to keep the fact that you helped build that team and that you build organizations, and you did it by being a great Talent Acquisition leader.

CONCLUSION

It has been my goal throughout this book to reveal the increasingly complex and challenging task faced by the organizational Talent Acquisition leader. Our industry has been transformed by the growing number of recruiting tools available today including: applicant and talent management technology, social media, online databases, online job marketing and job boards, and the globalization of many large companies. Talent Acquisition leaders are expected to understand and know how to lead a Talent Acquisition function across vast and decentralized global enterprises. Organizations expect true Talent Acquisition strategists who can really drive competitive value for the organization and "win" through talent.

To help move the talent management profession forward I've explored the important issues facing our industry including: workforce planning, metrics and economics of the internal Talent Acquisition organization; organizing, leading, and managing a consultative Talent Acquisition team; leading a proactive Talent Acquisition function that actually recruits; and organizational politics for the Talent Acquisition leader. I've discussed the power of relationships inside and outside the organization, as well as change management.

Perhaps most importantly, I've tried to emphasize that in today's multicultural Talent Acquisition universe, leadership is global but recruiting is local. At the end of the day, regardless of how many new technologies you use, or how deftly you navigate your way through corporate politics, what it comes down to is finding the right person for the job. And to do that there is no substitute for Recruiters sitting down across from candidates, and looking them in the eye. As a Talent Acquisition leader, you know that to make the right job offer takes a combination of metrics, research, schmoozing, respectful interrogation, humility, political maneuvering, and not a little clairvoyance. It has been my goal to show you how to leverage the one-on-one skills that you possess, bring value to your organization, and meet or exceed their goals and yours.

I want to reiterate one last thing that I started the book with in my preface. *Talent Acquisition professionals are legit and a critical part of shaping the organization*, not only in terms of the skills being brought into the organization, but to the corporate culture. Talent Acquisition takes a human approach to marketing the company, be it through relationships with candidates, or the programs developed to inspire employees to share the positive experience they are having, thus encouraging others to want to join. Companies are run by people; any decent leader will confirm this, so Talent Acquisition is truly building the future. Say it out loud to yourself and your team, we have to believe in ourselves as professionals! Remember, you can be a STAR without being superhuman—we take a lot from business strategy, but also contribute to it. With the RecruitCONSULT! approach to Talent Acquisition, business leaders will continue to rely on our strategic support and continue to see the benefit through each and every employee.

INDEX

A

account management, 61–62
active candidate recruiting
    active and passive recruiting, balance between, 76–78
    active candidates, defining, 74
    in economic downturns, 114
    headhunting, 1, 3, 75
    job boards and, 80
    in Talent Acquisition Organization Maturity model, 4
algorithms, hiring by, 37–38
All-In RPO model, 87, 89, 94
allocation models for Talent Acquisition funding, 49–50
Application Tracking System (ATS)
    AI use and, 23, 24
    candidate search time, reducing, 25
    CRM, using with, 22
    efficiency metrics, acquiring through, 45
    email, exporting from, 132
    features and services, 29, 30
    global ATS cautions, 164–65
    in Japan, 169
    in the Philippines, 170
Artificial Intelligence (AI), 22–23
Asia-Pacific region, 152, 153, 168–72

B

best practices
    Client/Vendor model, no best practice sharing in, 64
    as cycling through with staff, 65
    as non-interchangeable, 41–42, 67
    Recruiters, sharing among, 66
    team involvement in creating, 181
biases
    candidate surveys and unbiased feedback, 44, 131

Made in the USA
Columbia, SC
14 March 2018